MODERN
LANDSCAPE
ARCHITECTURE

MODERN
LANDSCAPE
ARCHITECTURE

REDEFINING

THE

GARDEN

PHOTOGRAPHY BY
FELICE FRANKEL

TEXT BY
JORY JOHNSON

ABBEVILLE PRESS
PUBLISHERS
NEW YORK
LONDON
PARIS

Modern Landscape Architecture was supported in part by a grant from the National Endowment for the Arts, a federal agency.

FRONT COVER: The Wright House, Seattle, Washington, designed by architect Arthur Erickson and landscape architect Cornelia Hahn Oberlander.
BACK COVER: Weyerhaeuser Company Headquarters, designed by architect E. Charles Bassett (Skidmore, Owings & Merrill) and landscape architect Peter Walker.
HALF-TITLE PAGE: A tranquil spot in the Bloedel Reserve, Bainbridge Island, Washington.
TITLE PAGE: The Pinecote Pavilion, designed by architect Fay Jones, at the Crosby Arboretum, Picayune, Mississippi.
DEDICATION PAGE: Aquatic vegetation in the pond at the Crosby Arboretum.
CONTENTS PAGE: Paley Park, New York City, designed by Zion & Breen Associates, Inc.

EDITORS: Jacqueline Decter, Alison Mitchell, Constance Herndon
DESIGNER: Julie Rauer
COPY CHIEF: Robin James
PRODUCTION SUPERVISOR: Hope Koturo

Library of Congress Cataloging-in-Publication Data

Johnson, Jory.
     Modern landscape architecture : redefining the garden / photographs by Felice Frankel : text by Jory Johnson.
         p.   cm.
     Includes bibliographical references and index.
     ISBN 1-55859-023-4
     1. Landscape architecture—United States.   I. Frankel, Felice.
II. Title.
SB470.53.J64   1991
712'.0973—dc20   91-2740
                                                                                          CIP

First edition

CONTENTS

PHOTOGRAPHER'S REMARKS

"Space has always reduced me to silence."
—Jules Vallès, *L'Enfant*

The pictures in this book were taken over a period of five years. I visited all the sites a number of times, and each visit revealed to me another layer of meaning. An essential quality of their beauty is that there is always another layer.

I will never forget my first visit to the Salk Institute, for example. Some people find it sterile and cold. For me, it became a place of contemplation. The mental journey that you take while standing at the beginning of the water channel is a response to the brilliant use of space and materials. The horizon beckons you. Although you are standing two hundred feet away, you are connected to it. When you do finally walk the beam of water to the end, you discover you've been fooled. There is more there than you thought. Yet this discovery does not lessen the pleasure of a second visit; a knowledge of the complexity strengthens the elegance of design.

The places photographed were created with patience and with a cunning that has allowed time to intercede. Time affects landscape design more than any other design discipline. Growth changes scale and density. Seasons change palette. Moments change quality of light. The designer can only anticipate what is to be, but cannot control all that will be.

These photographs create their own reality. The choice of certain lenses and camera positions causes particular perspectives to emerge. In the framing, that which makes the image less comprehensible is edited out. In the end, three dimensions have, of course, become two. Yet in spite of all these subjective determinations, I ask the reader to trust the pictures. They were created as personal responses to these places, and all were taken from vantage points that can be experienced by others. Our decision to include a plan of each project freed me from the need to provide purely documentary pictures; it enabled me to inform in a different way.

I am grateful to the National Endowment for the Arts, whose generous grant made possible my many trips to the sites. I am indebted to the owners of the private gardens for their hospitality and understanding.

My thanks to Owen Hungerford, Richard Brown, and Ed Blake. And to David Shepherd, whose artistry and knowledge of horticulture are inspiring.

To Jackson, Vaclav Kalas, Tim Sanderson, Jack Schmeckibier, Roberta Sherman, Neill Whitman, and Harold Williams. I am grateful to Peter Atkins, Phil Bochetti, Christine Cottle, Joseph Hanson, Craig Mack, Jim McCulloch, and Charles T. Mason, Jr.

My thanks to my friends Lois Craig, Annick Porter, and Dennis Porter, who didn't let me get away with anything. To photographer and friend Ken Druse, who has been through it himself and kept me laughing.

To editors Constance Herndon, who began with us, Alison Mitchell, and Jackie Decter, who took us through to the end. All three brought intelligence and clarity to the project. To designer Julie Rauer, whose talent and unusual sensitivity brought another dimension to my photographs.

And finally to my sons, Matthew and Michael, and to my husband, Ken, who understood throughout all the months of my being away—or at least fooled me into that peace of mind.

PREFACE

The past forty years have been a prolific and vital period in landscape design, yet most of the work remains undocumented and unchronicled. *Modern Landscape Architecture* has been written to encourage critical consideration and evaluation of this important era, which changed our relationship to the natural and built landscape. As landscape architect Laurie Olin wrote about Richard Haag, Lawrence Halprin, Thomas Church, Dan Kiley, and other designers featured in the book, "Their work represents the first truly fresh developments (both stylistically and formally) since the late eighteenth century."[1]

Felice Frankel and I have chosen to concentrate on selected projects instead of presenting a *tour d'horizon*. This approach regretfully precludes discussion of some major landscape architects and designers, but the extended analysis of those included allows one to gain a deeper understanding of how landscapes are designed, constructed, and then redesigned through natural processes, habitation, and maintenance. Our approach also differs significantly from texts that consider the larger physical contexts of design projects—particularly urban ones—at the expense of the more detailed aspects of the built environment. Our criteria for the selection of specific projects included not only the intrinsic merit of the design and its successful maturation, but also the social and philosophical ideas that have made the work an expression of its time.

Since *Modern Landscape Architecture* features all original photography, the projects had to be in excellent physical condition, a criterion that unfortunately excluded some historically important landscapes. However, the photographs offer far more than mere documentation; they are also critical visual essays that illuminate the nuances and poetic qualities of the designs at different times of year.

Surprisingly, there were no existing plans for a number of these projects and many previously published plans were inaccurate. The plans in *Modern Landscape Architecture* are our interpretation of the resolution between the designer's intentions and the actual construction of the design (as the essays in the book make clear, there is many a slip between the designer's pencil and the laborer's shovel). Occasionally, we have included significant unrealized portions of a design and, in other cases, we have not included recent alterations, especially if they involve only minor planting changes.

Every landscape design is a complex collaboration involving—to varying degrees—the client, the landscape architect, the architect, the engineers, and other professionals and nonprofessionals. We apologize for any important contributions to these projects that we may have inadvertently overlooked in the text or the project credits.

As recently as the nineteenth century, especially in England, theories and polemics on politics, social order, economics, and our relationship to nature were expressed through landscape or garden design. Before undertaking an important project a landscape designer would consider not only architectural and horiticultural history and practice, but also contemporaneous politics, poetry, and the fine arts. Now the general public and even many critics and professionals resist thinking about landscape design as an expression of an idea or belief—in fact, most books on the subject include only physical descriptions—preferring to assume an innocent appreciation of physical sensations. The landscape has become a place to escape speculation and intellectual stimulation. *Modern Landscape Architecture* is an attempt to return the landscape to the service of the intellect as well as the senses.

Among the many people who helped with this project, Felice Frankel and I would like to thank the following: for initial encouragement and letters of support, William Howard Adams, Cheryl Barton, John Beardsley, Paul Friedberg, Richard Haag, Duke Johns, Laurie Olin, Peter Walker, and John G. Williams.

For reading drafts of the book, helping to

narrow the list of projects, and refining thematic ideas, we would like to thank Diana Balmori, Warren Byrd, Patrick Condon, Lois Craig, Garrett Eckbo, Lawrence Halprin, George Hargreaves, Charles Harris, Kenneth Helphand, Catherine Howett, Linda Jewell, Debra Karasov, Steve Krog, Phil Morris, James Rose, Robert Royston, Hideo Sasaki, Martha Schwartz, Anne Spirn, Mark Treib, Michael Van Valkenburgh, and John Wong, as well as all those acknowledged in the text.

For reviewing the manuscript and offering valuable suggestions to improve its clarity and focus, I am indebted to Elizabeth Meyers, Skip Burck, Jot Carpenter, and Melanie Simo.

I wish to thank my former colleagues at the University of North Carolina at Charlotte, College of Architecture, particularly Eric Sauda, Michael Swisher, and Deborah Ryan for their support and often unknowing contributions to the text.

Many thanks to editors Constance Herndon, Alison Mitchell, and Jackie Decter. Special thanks to my wife, Margaret Cheniae, without whose preliminary editing Constance, Alison, and Jackie's job would have gone from difficult to impossible.

Finally, Felice and I are grateful to Hong Choe for most of the plan drawings and to Kelly Stribling for those of Becton Dickinson, Gas Works Park, and PepsiCo.

INTRODUCTION

Modern American landscape designers have produced a vast body of original, innovative, and beautiful work that can be read today as a powerful expression of the cultural, economic, and social adaptations of postwar American life. Although influenced by early-twentieth-century modernism, these designers did not share the European avant-garde's rejection of bourgeois values, but instead sought to ennoble the working environments and public spaces of middle-class Americans.

The *retardataire* revival era that preceded American modernism was frustrating for many designers because of the contemporaneous achievements of the European avant-garde. In the 1920s, American landscape architect Fletcher Steele wrote enthusiastically about the modern French landscape architects Gabriel Guévrékian, André and Paul Véra, and Pierre Legrain, whose designs were highly influenced by cubism. Steele hoped that modern garden design would "bring a new meaning into the whole contemporaneous movement of thought and art" but knew that his wealthy, conservative American clients expected "tasteful and refined" gardens eclectically decorated with pergolas, fountains, and statuary. Steele, like many young landscape architects of the era, lamented, "We

gardeners have always been behind other artists in adopting new ideas."[1]

The revival period was something of an anomaly in the history of American design. In fact, modern landscape design has more in common with the ideas of nineteenth-century designers than with those of the early twentieth century. During the 1800s, America had been less bound by convention and was eager to find an appropriate expression for a young democratic nation. Led by Frederick Law Olmsted, landscape architects focused on moral and social issues. In his great naturalesque urban parks Olmsted adapted the English Garden as an engine of social reform, bringing the working-class citizens of New York into salubrious contact with rural scenery and fresh air. In architecture, the Chicago School favored invention, engineering, and originality over classicism, historicism, and conventionality.

Ironically, however, it was in Chicago, at the 1893 World's Columbian Exposition, that America turned away from progressive design. Dazzled by the "white city's" pastiche of imposing classical exhibition pavilions, Americans embraced the neoclassical revival for the next half century. Estate gardens featured Italianate, symmetrical designs, and in landscape architecture schools students learned to design "in the style of" French or Italian historical gardens. Maverick architects, such as Frank Lloyd Wright or the midwestern landscape architect Jens Jensen, argued for a regional prairie style and a recognition of the modern age, but won few mainstream followers.

The hegemony of the Beaux-Arts designers was broken in the 1930s by the arrival of Walter Gropius and other European refugees who had pioneered the International Style of design. Gropius had been one of the founders of the Bauhaus school in Germany, which stressed collaboration between designers and craftsmen and design for social utility. Since few jobs were available to professional architects during the Depression, Gropius and other charismatic designers and artists found teaching positions. In the late 1930s Gropius was chairman of the Architecture Department at Harvard when Garrett Eckbo, James Rose, and Dan Kiley were landscape architecture students there. Frustrated that the Landscape Architecture Department had not embraced modernism, the students published a series of seminal articles on a new paradigm of landscape design that would address the problems of modern urban life and the need to plan for America's population explosion. As Eckbo recalls, "Bremer Pond [a Harvard Professor] told me that there could be no modern landscape architecture because trees weren't made in factories. But we were living in a world that had airplanes, cars, radios, and new construction tools—why on earth were we still designing gardens in the style of the Tudors or Louis XIV? Or why did everything have to be either formal or informal—why couldn't a design have both?"[2]

But Eckbo and other early modernists were less interested in style than in addressing far more fundamental social and environmental problems, such as urbanization and suburban sprawl. Landscape architect Paul Friedberg designed playgrounds in inner city neighborhoods, while Eckbo designed housing for migrant workers and Lawrence Halprin tackled the problems of subsidized housing. They rejected the Beaux-Arts methodology, which held that there were ideal forms of organization for landscapes and buildings, and that these should be adapted to the site and the client's needs. Rather, they believed that designs should be a reflection of the client's and user's needs.

The eagerness of young designers to explore social and formal ideas in the landscape was not always shared by major architectural theorists. Architecture historian Henry-Russell Hitchcock, Jr., one of the champions of modern architecture, wrote that landscape design should consist of only "the simplest and most practical provisions for specific human needs" while preserving the "natural character of the site."[3] This reduced the landscape to serving as a pictorial or symbolic background for the building instead of possessing any spatial and experiential qualities of its own. Hitchcock's repeated use of the word "natural" betrayed an ecological naiveté, since most building sites were abandoned farmlands or second-growth forests. This uninformed romantic view of nature explains in part why landscape design never embraced two of the most innovative expressions of modern architects: the building's structure and the machine aesthetic.

Modern architecture espoused the idea of frankly expressing a building's structural system and even, in later years, of exposing the mechanical apparatus to achieve a new aesthetic that would have been unimaginable to earlier generations. But in the landscape, technological or structural expression was seldom, if ever, in evidence. A few landscape architects, such as Garrett Eckbo and James Rose, experimented with new materials such as aluminum and plastic, but by the 1950s landscape architects drew little inspiration from modern technology. Machines had become accepted facts—not avatars of a new era—and though buildings exposed previously hidden structures, the "structure" of a built landscape—the vast mechanical apparatus of drainage lines, irrigation systems, and foundations—remained hidden. Building systems had become "second nature," while outdoors, people wanted to experience an Edenic innocence away from technology.

Modern landscape design arose during the peak of America's postwar prosperity and self-confidence. When the economic restraints of the Great Depression and the war were removed, American industry harnessed the rational and technological aspects of European modernism to the ideology of capitalist expansion. America's unchallenged economic supremacy was celebrated in new, expansive corporate headquarters and office buildings, which gained dominion in pastoral suburban landscapes.

Young landscape architects, including Eckbo, Halprin, Thomas Church, and Robert Royston soon discovered that California, with its pioneering spirit and salubrious climate, was receptive to their new ideas. Their designs for upper-middle-class clients, including Church's Donnell Garden (pages 164–173), were asymmetrical, constructivist spatial organizations that allowed for a complex of activities. These clients were of the "baby-boom" generation, and the emphasis on family and home led designers to redefine the garden as, in Eckbo's phrase, a "landscape for living" that included sandboxes, children's jungle gyms, barbecue grills, swimming pools, small vegetable and cutting gardens, and deck chairs for cocktail parties. These innovations were more gradually accepted in the East, where leading designers such as A. E. Bye used native plants and indigenous materials in less obviously "modern" designs. In the Midwest and the South, modern gardens in the midst of Georgian and Colonial Revival houses and gardens became symbols of the owners' progressive or liberal views.

Landscape architect Peter Walker remembers being told as a student that: "Italian and French gardens were all built for decadent, authoritarian societies. Japanese Gardens were the only ones worth studying, except for maybe some English gardens . . ."[4] Aesthetically, designers were inspired by Japanese design principles such as asymmetry, contemplation, and suggestions of incompleteness and open-endedness. Landscape architects adapted these sensibilities to the larger scale of American projects by drawing from the dynamic compositions of modern abstract art, especially constructivism, surrealism, biomorphism, and geometrical abstraction.

By the early 1960s, Lawrence Halprin and others had carried their mastery of a personal, domestic, site-responsive design vocabulary into the public realm. Halprin's use of hard-edged, constructivist plinths, buttresses, and roaring water cascades for Ira's Fountain (pages 142–153) became a recognizable "signature style," contrasting sharply with both Olmstedian naturalesque parks and the classical ideals of the City Beautiful movement.

By the late 1960s, projects and budgets had grown in size. Landscape architectural firms became larger in order to tackle complex commissions including regional planning, new towns, urban redevelopment, college campuses, and transportation systems. Environmental impact statements, community review boards, long public review processes, and the teamwork and interdisciplinary coordination necessitated by large projects sometimes worked to suppress artistic expression by individual designers. However, this rapid evolution of modern landscape architecture was exhilarating for its principals. Stuart Dawson, lead designer for Deere & Company (pages 29–39), remembers, "We had to figure out everything for the first time. Nobody had built things like suburban corporate headquarters, commuter college campuses, or seaside resorts.'[5]

The amount of information that needed to be gathered and synthesized for larger projects sometimes left little time for site-specific design. Designers wanted to reinforce *une pensée mère*—a "mother thought" or main idea—and paid less attention to artistic detailing and small-scale design. The unfortunate legacy are a great many faceless plazas, campuses, and office complexes. But in the best modern projects, as in the best abstract art, carefully considered details such as those at the Salk Institute (pages 226–235) give the main idea tactility and suggest a metaphysical, spiritual dimension.

Some of the best site-specific designs of this period were for corporations whose officers devoted additional time and energy to the design development of their headquarters and other major projects. Corporations had the money and the will to construct and maintain ambitious designs. In telling contrast, many of the public plazas and parks built in the 1960s were ravaged by the recessions and energy crises of the late 1970s.

It is important to bear in mind that no built

landscape is ideologically neutral. Aesthetic considerations can never be separated entirely from the economic and political realities of their era. The landscape designs shown here cannot be understood apart from the constraints of market conditions, consumer demand, and their dependence on the late-capitalist ideology that has allowed them to endure.

By the 1980s, America's confidence had been eroded by the Vietnam War, economic recessions, the recognition of environmental dilemmas, and intractable social and urban problems. The superb landscape designs of previous decades were barely visible amid the vast expanse of thoughtless and rapacious development. Planners began returning to older town patterns and symmetrical classical designs—the kind first favored by Americans seeking to carve a civilization from a hostile wilderness. Landscape architects such as Martha Schwartz, George Hargreaves, Ron Wiggington, Lee Weintraub, Laurie Olin, and Michael Van Valkenburg began to employ fragmentation (design features not obviously integrated into a balanced, harmonious composition), historical quotation, and explicit regionalism—all strategies anathema to pure modernism. Their designs, as well as those by environmental artists, made the average modern landscape design seem "despite its technical and functional merits . . . aesthetically and sensuously barren."[6] Some landscape architects who embraced the ecological imperatives of the environmental movement denounced geometrical designs as "elitist aestheticism."[7] Such statements accurately describe the banal imitations of the icons of modernism but do not account for the truly original and remarkable achievements of the era. The statements also remind us that in the voracious building boom of the period, the work of the masters was vastly outnumbered by facile imitations.

Today, though many landscape architects are still building on modernism's achievements, it has clearly become a historic period, preceded by the neoclassical revival of the first half of the twentieth century and superseded by the pluralism and ecological mandates of the century's latter decades. But it is not a well-defined or well-documented period. As professor of landscape architecture Elizabeth Meyers recently complained, "There's almost no literature on modern landscape design, which makes it very difficult for students and professionals to know their own history."[8] With few exceptions, practicing landscape architects used to publish their work under the guise of instructional guidebooks for homeowners—thereby restricting their discussion of design to an elementary level—instead of writing more ambitious theoretical books for colleagues and students. The leading journal of the profession, Landscape Architecture, published little contemporary design because, as Grady Clay, the journal's editor from 1959–1984, explains, "I took the firm position that the magazine should look to the future, to unexplored territory, not to celebrate what was being done. . . . I published [Ian] McHarg's work before landscape architects had even heard of ecological planning and I published earth artists and cultural geographers writing about vernacular landscapes. . . . Most of the work that landscape architecture firms were doing was pedestrian, repetitious, and unimaginative and I didn't think it was worth publishing."[9] Even the American Society of Landscape Architects award winners were published in the back pages of the journal if at all, rendering the best work of the profession so invisible that it could not attain the iconic status and authority necessary to mobilize the new generation. Today, with a resurgence of interest in modernism, historians and practicing landscape architects are finally beginning to fill the void in the literature of the profession.

It is still too early to read the modern era clearly, but this book is a beginning of a reassessment of modern landscape design. It will have succeeded if some of the best designs of the era are revealed in all their mastery and sensual delight.

ONE

TRADITION AND INVENTION

In *The Shape of Time,* art historian George Kubler explores the process of artistic change and defines the difference between what he calls "prime objects," which involve radical invention, and "replicas," which make small adjustments to existing artistic models. Any art form's potential innovation is "narrowly limited by the existing state of knowledge." Kubler further distinguishes between instrumental or practical inventions and aesthetic inventions. The latter "enlarge human awareness directly with new ways of experiencing the universe, rather than with new objective interpretations."[1]

More than any other artistic genre, landscape design appeals to preconceived images. Because plants usually mature slowly and are less conducive to formal manipulations than building materials or most artistic mediums, landscape design is not as well-equipped as painting, literature, music, or even architecture to reflect the rapid changes of modern culture. The intrinsic conservatism of landscape design was noted by Francis Bacon in 1625: ". . . when Ages grow to Civility and Elegancie, Men come to Build Stately, sooner than to Garden Finely: As if Gardening were the Greater Perfection."[2]

Architects and landscape architects usually serve long apprenticeships in established firms and then take years to build their own practice. They generally do not build major works until they are middle aged, which can

engender a certain conservatism. Russell Page's work at PepsiCo is in many ways a grand summation of his own career, as well as of the long tradition of English landscape gardening. The naturalistic landscape at Deere & Company is an equally powerful example of an equally venerable pastoral tradition. And in both cases, the projects were strongly determined by the clients' desire to commission traditional landscapes even as they embraced modern architecture and office design.

Landscape design that denies Kubler's "radical invention" appeals to those who want to use the landscape to "get away from it all." But however much one might want to consider the landscape an immaculate arena in which intellectual ideas and political and economic systems do not operate, it is impossible for landscape designs to be concerned purely with surface aesthetics or formal properties. Designers must accept responsibility for their formal decisions because forms are always laden with meaning, whether or not the meaning is intentional. The difficulty with designs that unreflectively perpetuate pastoral landscapes, imitation Japanese gardens, or caricatures of natural landscapes lies not in their formal execution, but in the fact that the forms are of a different time and connect with neither the immediate architecture nor the contemporary world at large. They are, in Kubler's terms, finely crafted replicas instead of prime objects.

It is futile to assume that traditions are completely irrelevant, though some modern designers have tried—it simply isn't possible not to know the past. Only through reference to precedents and traditions can genuine invention be recognized. Modern designers seldom refer to precedents or use direct historical quotation, but, as evidenced by the designs in this section, they simultaneously transform historical forms and invent new forms appropriate to the zeitgeist. By their use of tradition and invention, they seek to shape an authentic physical identity for their own time. These designs are to be judged by the authenticity of their invention, not by the authority of the past.

PEPSICO

**PURCHASE
NEW YORK**

One of the all too frequent failings of modern architecture and landscape architecture has been an emphasis on functional planning at the expense of a particular vision for the site and the client. When it was completed in 1970, PepsiCo World Headquarters stood in a pastoral landscape with a large lake and a great expanse of lawn, all framed by second-growth New England woods. But what an *Architectural Record* critic called "a skillful interplay of buildings and open spaces, of created and natural areas"[1] seemed to PepsiCo CEO Donald Kendall aesthetically empty. The response of a company dedicated to consumerism was to fill that perceived vacuum with collections of sculpture and plants. After twenty years, PepsiCo's landscape is now an uneasy mixture of stolid modernist architecture, strong site planning, and a large garden filled with sculpture and horticultural incidents.

The evolution of PepsiCo's landscape began with Edward Durell Stone, Sr. (1902–1978), a "classical" modernist architect whose symmetrical structures were usually covered with decorative grilles or ornamental patterns. Stone's son, landscape architect Edward D. Stone, Jr. (1932–   ), was responsible for the site planning and worked closely with his father on the development of the architectural massing. His firm, Edward D. Stone, Jr. & Associates, is best known for its large-scale planning, coastal management, and new communities; and like his father, Ed Stone, Jr., is a committed modernist more interested in social and environmental issues than in detailed artistic expression.

PepsiCo's 112-acre site was a former polo field surrounded by second-growth forest. Zoning

Robert Davidson's *Totems* (1986) stand amid dawn redwoods.

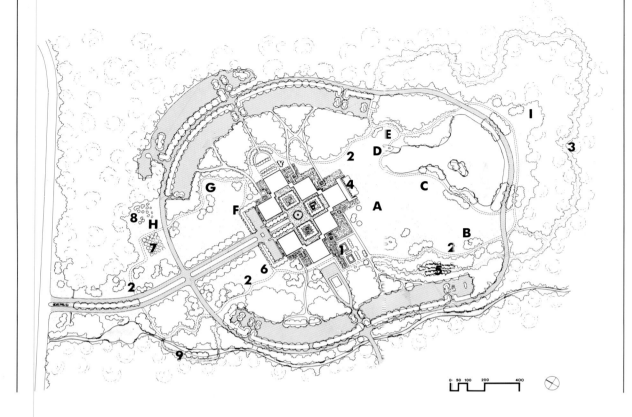

regulations prohibiting high-rise buildings led Stone Sr. to design seven three-story pavilions, one for each of PepsiCo's seven product divisions. These are lined at the corners with stairways and elevators and, in the interior, define three sunken courtyards. This arrangement is illustrative of Stone's classicist desire for symmetry, but it could become problematic if PepsiCo were to reorganize its divisions.

The site slopes down from the entrance to the existing polo field and Stone Jr. used the slope to advantage by constructing large, ivy-covered berms that conceal the storage and mechanical systems. Though most corporate employees—especially in New England—prefer a short walk to their cars, Stone Jr. wanted to avoid putting large parking lots next to the building. Instead, he spread the parking among the trees on either side of the open field and linked the two lots with a one-mile ring road. "Since it added fifty to one hundred yards to the walk, I was afraid they wouldn't go for it," Stone remembers, "but Donald Kendall said, 'Let them walk. We'll make the walk interesting enough so they'l forget how far they're walking.'"[2]

During preliminary excavation, an underground spring was discovered, and this was used to create an artificial lake. Even during dry summers the spring has kept the water level constant. Stone Jr.'s pastoral design[3] for the lake included a rock outcropping, overhanging willows, and enough contour manipulation so that the entire body of water can never be seen in a single glance. The proportions of the lake to the lawn area are almost equal, but viewed from the dining room terrace, the lawn appears much larger. However, PepsiCo's Donald Kendall soon found another use for the spacious lawn.

Kendall was very concerned with employee satisfaction after the corporation's move from Manhattan to Purchase, New York, and the new headquarters was to provide many amenities, including one of the first complete employee fitness centers—perhaps insuring that employees would be able to walk the extra one hundred yards to their cars. Kendall wanted an environment that would "reflect the essential qualities of corporate success, ranging from stability to adventure."[4] An art collector himself, the CEO felt that PepsiCo's success could best be reflected by a lushly landscaped park and a collection of modern sculpture.

Earlier in the century, American banks had built classical temples for their main branches, in part to reflect their wealth and to prove that good public relations—including contributing to the city's physical image—were more important than the lucrative rentable space of a commercial skyscraper (an attitude long since abandoned by most American banks). Today PepsiCo's richly landscaped grounds and blue-chip sculpture collection demonstrate the corporation's financial success, commitment to the public welfare, and its "stability and adventure." It is interesting to note that PepsiCo's rival, Coca-Cola, also began creating an impressive sculpture park in the 1970s at its headquarters in Atlanta. PepsiCo encourages visitors, offering color brochures identifying the sculptures and the main areas of horticultural interest.

PepsiCo sells fast food to the average consumer, and its enterprises include Kentucky Fried Chicken, Taco Bell, Frito-Lay, and, of course, Pepsi-Cola. Equally important to PepsiCo's corporate health is the stock it sells to financially secure individuals or corporate investors. PepsiCo's sculpture collection is cleverly poised between the two client groups: there are valuable abstract sculptures

The ornamental grass garden near the entrance to the main courtyard. The same area has a collection of flowering trees that bloom in spring soon after the grasses have been cut back to allow for new growth.

The pastoral lake curves around weeping willows. Bald cypress has been planted behind the lake.

by Henry Moore, Isamu Noguchi, Alexander Calder, Auguste Rodin, and David Smith, but the most centrally located sculptures are a sentimental bear and a playful dolphin by British sculptor David Wynne. While the Wynnes aren't likely to appreciate as fast as the canonical moderns, they are the most popular with visitors, especially the busloads of schoolchildren who visit the grounds each year. The sculpture collection continues to grow, but like PepsiCo, leans more toward stability than adventure. However, its conservatism, particularly its resistance to the consensus among contemporary artists and critics that public art should be either functional or site specific, reflects Kendall's personal taste—"I don't think that environmental artists would fit into the collection, though I might have a couple of them do something in the natural areas away from the main grounds"[5]—and the collection may take a new direction with a future CEO, though probably not a radically different one.

After the building opened in 1970, the sculpture collection was initiated with a monumental Calder and Henry Moore's *Double Oval*. During the early 1970s, Stone Jr. had no idea the collection would grow to over forty major pieces, but he soon found himself reacting to new acquisitions with ad hoc decisions on their siting. Yet Stone's large office practice left him little time for continual detailed tinkering with sculptures and plantings, and after ten years Kendall found a more kindred spirit in the British garden designer Russell Page (1906–1985).

Over his long career Page had designed hundreds of private gardens for the wealthy elite of Europe. He viewed his work as timeless, as far removed from questions of modernism as his gardens were from the public gaze. Page was relentlessly inventive, and his work was marred only by occasional overcomplication. PepsiCo was his opportunity to create a final public legacy for a client as committed and wealthy as any European aristocrat. Page devoted himself to PepsiCo's "corporate villa" from 1981 until his death from cancer in 1985.

Stone Jr. worked briefly with Page, but soon withdrew. "We had different orientations. Russell was a genius about plants and he saw plants as being an end in themselves, whereas I viewed plants as defining spaces. I wanted to create a unified composition and had worked towards creating definite spaces. PepsiCo has summer concerts and other public events and we designed the grounds to preserve the flexible open spaces for these and any other events PepsiCo might sponsor. Page thought it needed more episodes and smaller spaces and began putting trees in the spaces. Finally, we withdrew and the grounds became more of an arboretum than we had envisioned."[6]

Page thought that Stone's plan "had good bones" but needed a more clearly directed circulation and a greater variety of effects. He began staking out the "Golden Path," a serpentine, five-foot-wide path of amber-colored pebbles known as "chocolate stone" in the trade. The approximately one-and-three-quarter-mile path makes one loop around the building and a smaller loop around the lake. Although visitors can walk off the path and make their way across the lawn, the PepsiCo guidebook encourages first-time visitors to stay on the path, which leads to all the important sculptures and horticultural features. The path is insistent in its own dimension and never becomes an edge—even when it parallels the woods, there are always at least four or five feet of lawn between the path and the woodland ground cover. The only break occurs at the rock outcropping on which Wynne's bear kneels. Page's planning was indeed meticulous: Full-scale mock-ups were ordered of each new sculpture, and Kendall marveled at the hours Page spent positioning stakes for the new trees, moving them back and forth a few feet (and sometimes only a foot or even less) until he was completely satisfied.

There is no curatorial sequence to the path: to follow it is to experience the landscape through the eyes of one of our century's master gardeners, seeing textures, colors, and compositions of trees, shrubs, and sculptures slowly unfold so each can be fully appreciated and photographed before the path turns and presents the next scene. The peripatetic experience is more scenic than spatial—visitors are led alongside the bosque of birch trees instead of through them.

Page had an almost mystical sense of objects in landscapes. In his autobiography he wrote: "My understanding is that every object emanates—sends out vibrations beyond its physical body which are specific to itself. These vibrations vary with the nature of the object, the materials it is made of, its colour, its textures, and its form."[7] When it came to sculpture, Page had a wonderful feel for each piece, but he didn't really like modern sculpture, and had little interest in its underlying meaning and aesthetic concepts. He once remarked: "I use the trees as sculptures and the sculptures as flowers and then I take it from there."[8] Kendall, too, is primarily concerned with visual effects: "Sometimes we might try to keep artists of the same period together, but mostly we position the sculptures where they look best."[9]

This abdication of an overall curatorial responsibility can trivialize the collection. A sculpture park is like a museum show that brings together works from different collections. By placing one sculpture next to another or in sequence, a curator can lead the viewer to new insights and understandings. But from the dining room terrace at PepsiCo, Arnaldo Pomodoro's fifty-foot eroded columns, Wynne's *Grizzly Bear,* and Calder's bright red stabile look like uncomfortable guests at a cocktail party who have nothing to say to one another.

Stone Jr., like most modern landscape architects, tried to locate the sculpture advantageously in relationship to the land. Page disliked Stone's practice of letting the sculpture appear to sit directly

Isamu Noguchi's *Energy Void* (1974).

Weeping willows complete the serenity of the pastoral lake. The base of the building is bermed to hide mechanical services and storage.

on the ground, an attractive alternative once nylon grass whips made concrete mowing strips obsolete. Page favored planting a firm backdrop, such as the row of blue spruce behind the huge Calder. For other sculptures, he created a special horticultural base, such as the sharply incised bed of black Japanese mondograss (*Ophiopogon japonicos* "Ebony Knight") beneath Louise Nevelson's black steel *Celebration II*.

The difficulty with such care and feeding of sculpture is that a great deal of modern art is impolite and Page's genteel settings can turn the works into mere garden ornament. Jackson Pollock's paintings were most powerful when they filled entire walls of Peggy Guggenheim's house, but in the large rooms of modern museums, they are reduced to easel paintings. Abstract sculpture, with its rich, hard surfaces and aggressive scale, can sometimes be experienced best in an enforced and unexpected intimacy, but PepsiCo's landscape often acts as a kind of palliative for the more obdurate and disturbing art. The two atavistic figures of Max Ernst's *Capricorn* are evocative of dark rituals and nightmares, but Page's tidy ground cover and border fence transform them into an eccentric English couple on a park bench. If the landscape

The trees along the Golden Path frame a view of Alexander Calder's red *Hats Off* (1969) and Henry Moore's *Double Oval* (1967) in the distance.

The Golden Path leads to Claus Oldenburg's *Giant Trowel II* (1982) and George Segal's *Three People on Four Benches* (1979). In this context, one wonders if the third object is a fire hydrant or another sculpture.

design were to engage the sculpture as the best museum architecture does, it might revivify the sculpture's visceral intensity and meaning.

When he wasn't dealing directly with the sculpture, Page seemed more himself. It may have been that his sense of impending mortality during the final years of his life caused him to veer erratically between sublime distillations of his long career and eccentric horticultural follies that compete with the sculpture like rambunctious children.

There are many design passages at PepsiCo that will be magnificent as they mature. Along the far end of the lake, Page planted two drifts of

deciduous conifers, each containing forty to fifty trees planted very closely, about nine feet apart. One group is comprised of dawn redwoods (*Metasequoia glyptostroboides*), which are native to China, while the other group is of bald cypress (*Taxodium distichum*), native to the southern United States. The dawn redwood was first described from fossils and a living specimen wasn't discovered until 1944. It grows to over one hundred feet and its needles and exfoliating bark are similar to that of the bald cypress. Both trees are normally used as specimens, especially in New England where they are distinctly non-native. In time these two masses

will be as powerful as any of the sculptures. Page also left some domestic touches. Next to the service entrance is a small formal garden of three lily ponds and a glorious gray perennial border (which PepsiCo has carefully maintained and replanted as necessary).

Few could bring as much to the party as Russell Page, but there are some inspirations one would rather he had left at home. His grouping of topiary yews next to the lily pond looks like a bad imitation of abstract sculpture. A bosque of different species of birch trees intersected by diagonal mowing strips was a wonderful idea, but is too recondite as placed on the ring road next to the curious "gold garden," a collection of low golden conifers with Tony Smith's *Duck* sited uncomfortably *in medias res*.

Since Page's death, his assistant, François Goffinet, has continued to develop the site. Goffinet's primary task has been to frame the fastidious sculpture grounds and lake with naturalized plantings and woodland paths on the outside of the ring road. Goffinet has developed both the interstitial areas between the parking lots and the sculpture grounds, and the lower areas beyond the loop. The lower areas, many of which are seasonally damp or traversed by streams, are richly planted with perennials and native woodland species. These additional trails are especially popular with joggers and vigorous walkers.

Like a giant corporation, the landscape of PepsiCo is an amalgamation of different divisions and products. Unlike a corporation, however, its assets cannot be calculated simply by totaling up the profit of its individual parts. Considered singly, the classically symmetrical architecture and site plan, the robust adventures of modern sculpture, the planterly compositions, and the English landscape park and arboretum have value, but as a corporate entity they are far less successful than PepsiCo itself is.

Water lilies in one of the lily ponds designed by Russell Page.

PROJECT: **PEPSICO, INC.**

CLIENT: **PEPSICO, INC.**

DATE OF COMPLETION: **1970 (BUILDING)**

LOCATION: **PURCHASE, NEW YORK**

ARCHITECT: **EDWARD DURELL STONE & ASSOCIATES**

LANDSCAPE ARCHITECT: **EDWARD D. STONE, JR. & ASSOCIATES**
PROJECT LANDSCAPE ARCHITECT: **JOE LALLI**

LANDSCAPE DESIGNER: **RUSSELL PAGE: 1981—85**
FRANÇOIS GOFFINET: 1985—PRESENT

GENERAL CONTRACTOR: **TURNER CONSTRUCTION**

SITE ENGINEER: **GOODFRIEND-OSTERGAARD ASSOCIATES**

DEERE & COMPANY

M O L I N E
I L L I N O I S

In his book *The Machine in the Garden* historian Leo Marx proposes that America has struggled to reconcile a passion for the power and independence of the machine with a Jeffersonian love and nostalgia for a pastoral landscape. Americans dream that the two antinomies can be reconciled in a "middle landscape," an ideal landscape free from brutish machines, from the rawness and smell of working farms, and from the danger and hardships of untamed wilderness.[1] The landscape design of Deere & Company is the epitome of the "machine in the garden." It represents a middle ground: modern in spirit, but conservative in its horizon of aesthetic expectation.

In 1968 architect Eero Saarinen criticized mainstream contemporary architecture as "too humble. It should be prouder, more aggressive, much richer and larger." And Saarinen himself tried "to boldly express in architecture the special character of Deere & Company."[2] Left unfulfilled, however, was an opportunity for the landscape design to express that special character or its relationship to the natural world. The landscape design by Sasaki Associates, though validated by its sophisticated visual accord with Saarinen's building and its smooth disposition of sites and services, seems to ignore the building's bold, aggressive expression of the nature of Deere & Company, the nature of machines, and the nature of the technology and culture of its time.

Instead, the landscape celebrates a pastoral ideal—the harmony of human beings and nature. It is the land as it is imagined to have been before the plow, before section lines gridded the prairie.

Eero Saarinen's building completes the structure of the valley landscape.

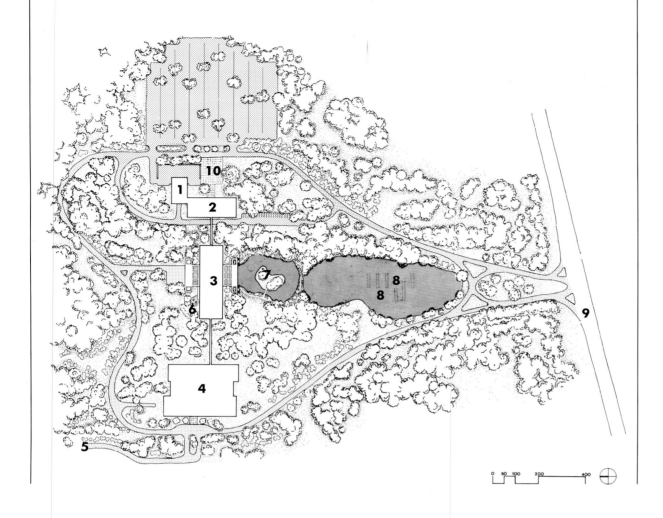

It is the romantic repository of the American birthright that the machine forever erased. In fact, it is the ideal landscape before the arrival of John Deere in 1833.

When John Deere came to Illinois from Vermont, he brought his new invention: a self-scouring plow that shed the sticky prairie loam and turned a precise furrow. By 1847, using imported steel from England, John Deere's company was producing over a thousand plows a year at his factory in Moline. In 1955, after a century of continued growth and expansion, Deere & Company decided to move their headquarters from downtown Moline to the rural countryside.

The locale itself is another kind of middle landscape—an ecotone between the geometrized Illinois farmland and the rolling hill country near the Mississippi River. After looking over the 450-acre site,[3] Saarinen designed an inverted pyramid

on top of a ridge overlooking the valley. Not altogether convinced, Deere's Chairman and CEO William Hewitt asked Saarinen how he planned to handle the company's theater, cafeteria, and possible future expansion. Saarinen puffed on his pipe and went back to his office in Bloomfield Hills, Michigan.[4]

Soon afterward, Saarinen visited Japan. When he returned, he tossed aside his plans for the inverted pyramid and started over. Using a model of the existing site, he began putting steel frame buildings down in the valley among the trees. Architect Paul Kennon, who worked with Saarinen on Deere, observes: "It came out of his visit to Japan. . . . It is a very romantic building . . . absolutely in sympathy with the trees."[5] The parking was above the buildings, on the site of the late but unlamented inverted pyramid.[6]

It was indeed a romantic building for a

A path winds around the
upper lake.

romantically disposed site—a long valley whose bottom land sloped southward between low cups of hills and flowed visually across the highway into Illinois farm fields. To the north, the head of the valley was too distant and obscured by trees to terminate it visually. Sasaki Associates worked with Saarinen to site the building so that it bridged the valley and locked the landscape into a firm composition. Sasaki Associates used different colored balloons to test the height and location of the building until it perfectly complemented the existing structure of the valley.

Saarinen had three goals: "First, to provide functional, efficient space which would take care of future expansion in flexible ways; second, to create a pleasant and appropriate environment for employees; and third, to express in architecture the special character of Deere & Co. . . . Farm machinery is not slick, shiny metal but forged iron and steel in big, forceful, functional shapes. The proper character for its headquarters should likewise not be a slick, precise, glittering glass and spindly metal building, but a building which is bold and direct, using metal in a strong, basic way."[7]

The dark Cor-ten steel columns echo the stout trunks of the deciduous trees.

The architecture's boldness and directness are reinforced by Saarinen's use of crimson-brown Cor-ten steel for the building's frame and projecting sun screen. Cor-ten steel, a high-tension corrosion-resistant alloy, was developed in the 1930s for building railroads. After an initial weathering, the steel stops rusting and bakes a protective surface that resists further deterioration. The material of choice for many modern sculptors, most prominently Richard Serra, Cor-ten steel is particularly beautiful in the countryside, where it merges with the earth tones of oaks and ashes, especially in the fall. In urban buildings, steel must be encased in concrete or applied as ornament because it weakens in a fire. But, far from city fire codes, Saarinen was able to dramatize and romanticize Deere's steel beams and members.

Completed in 1964, the new headquarters coincided with an important expansion at Deere & Company. During the 1960s and 1970s, new technology encouraged the growth of large-scale agribusiness, which accelerated the decline of the small family farm. While responding to the increasing demand for enormous tractors and harvesters, Deere was also expanding into financial services and the yard and lawn market.

Hewitt had wanted a building that was both memorable and comfortable in order to attract and hold good personnel, "a matter of critical importance to an international business located in a small

The juxtaposition of the bold steel structure and the romantic landscape snaps both sharply into focus.

midwestern city." After a full-scale mock-up of a building section had been created, Hewitt had to placate not only alarmed engineers who said, "We've been warning farmers against rust for 120 years and now Hewitt wants to build a big rusty building," but also those who worried that the modern headquarters would offend farmers and rural salesmen.

To allay such potential objections, the landscape was designed as a modern pastoral, a tradition that dates back to sixteenth-century Venice. A pastoral landscape is more than a pleasing rural scene, its theme is human beings living in simple harmony with the natural world. In Venetian pastoral landscapes, a kind of "middle landscape" that was neither wild nor urban was populated with shepherds or poets. It was an idyllic world infused with emotional, amorous, and nostalgic longings for a reconciliation between the world of cities and commerce and the wilderness. Modern pastoral art no longer relies on classical references, but instead uses modern images of human beings and nature. The meaning of the pastoral clearly resides in the human reference, though not necessarily in human

The rectangular spray fountains in the lower lake cool the water for the building's air-conditioning system. They are only operated during warmer weather.

Henry Moore's *Hill Arches,* seen from the executive dining room.

figures. At Deere & Company, the most effective human references are the steel columns that stand in the landscape among the dark tree trunks. In fact, the entire building might be taken as the human reference and the landscape harmonizes with the visual facts of the buildings, such as the dark steel posts and rust-colored guard rails. But except for the image of irrigation and utility in the rectangular jets of the lower lake, little or nothing connects to agriculture, farm machinery, or Deere's aggressive corporate expansion. In other words, the landscape is part of a much older tradition than

the modernity of the architecture might suggest.

Deere's employees cross over the landscape on an elevated entry plaza. They enter the building through a mammoth display center housing giant tractors and harvesters, walk across a steel bridge, and then take great delight in looking out at the natural landscape.[8] Those who disliked the modern building could look past the steel to a popular pastoral landscape. If the architecture challenged, the landscape design would ingratiate.

Few farmers are Luddites. Deere's dependable combines and tractors have liberated farmers and greatly enhanced their comfort and material status. Farmers' acceptance of the steel building may derive from their experience that technology is a democratic vehicle for the pursuit of happiness and that the garden—Deere's romantic landscape—is where they take their rest. How much this pastoral landscape smoothed the way for the building is incalculable, but it is clear that midwestern farmers were enthusiastic, joining architects and tourists in seeking out the remote award-winning headquarters. Over 300,000 visitors signed the guest register in the first decade.

Saarinen never saw Deere & Company. He died suddenly at the age of fifty-one just before construction began. His associates, Kevin Roche and John Dinkeloo, who later formed their own firm, completed the Administrative Building and in 1978 designed the West Office Building to Saarinen's master plan. Deere & Company also indefinitely retained Sasaki Associates, whose principal, Stuart Dawson, notes: "There is not one Deere executive who was there when we 'did it.' It's fun from time to time to catch them up on their own history."[9]

Founded in the early 1950s by Hideo Sasaki (1919–   ), Sasaki Associates became the model for professional landscape architecture practice after World War II. Sasaki hired architects, ecologists, planners, and engineers, as well as landscape architects, to create interdisciplinary teams to tackle large environmental issues: urban rehabilitation, new communities, regional highways and transportation systems, and new college campuses. The scale and quantity of the firm's projects, as well as its emphasis on empirical data and larger ecological and social issues, led to a team approach meant to generate a range of possible solutions. Sasaki Associates had no interest in developing a signature style and tried to find solutions that were pragmatic, socially useful, and visually pleasing for the client. Stuart Dawson (1935–   ), Sasaki Associates' partner-in-charge for Deere & Company, regarded the eclecticism of Sasaki Associates—made possible by employing many landscape architects with different styles—as a marketing advantage, explaining, "If someone wants a formal garden, we can do a formal garden. If people want buildings in spaces arranged in an English style, no problem . . . if the topography doesn't fit that solution, we'll do something else. . . . I think it's fair to say that you can't 'spot' a Sasaki project, but if you look carefully at our projects, you'll see a consistency in the scale, proportions, materials, and the way that people use the spaces. Frankly, it's too bad more designs aren't approached this way instead of [each project] having its individual landscape stamp—no matter where the location."[10]

Sasaki's goal for Deere & Company was to "enhance the beauty and character of the main buildings while minimizing the impact of roads, parking, and service buildings."[11] Stuart Dawson described the existing site as "somewhat derelict. The Dutch elm disease had just hit and over a thousand elms were dead or dying. There were some old apple trees and some grazing, but mostly it was too steep to farm. The soil was hard clay with very poor drainage."[12] Sasaki Associates planted well over a thousand trees and shrubs, many to compensate for the lost elms. The planting design is visually but not scientifically indigenous; all the trees and shrubs "look native"—meaning that evergreens and other obvious exotics were proscribed—and they were planted according to their horticultural requirements: red maples in the low areas, oaks on the side slopes, and sugar maples on the high, well-drained areas. The decision to have an all-deciduous landscape that still had presence in the winter was not easy to achieve, especially since Deere officials thought any problems with sight lines or foundations could be quickly solved with a few evergreens.

Saarinen had wanted the building to be a bridge, but it cannot avoid being a dam, especially since Saarinen designed the executive dining room on the ground floor instead of the penthouse so that it would have a very dramatic view from just *below* the water level. Since the gentle valley is quite large, there is a tremendous watershed on the north side of the building. Sasaki Associates had to use a series of siltation basins and a 108-inch culvert to take the water around the building and into the lower lake. The upper lake is adjacent

The elevated walkway between the Administration Building and the West Wing Office Building.

Deere's romantic landscape is a modern version of the pastoral landscape.

to the building and uses city water, which allows for greater control of silting and flooding. So the executive dining room has a year-round view of water; the upper lake is aerated to improve the water quality for the goldfish and to keep the lake from freezing during the winter months. The lower lake serves as flood control and as a heat-exchange vehicle for the air-conditioning system—rectangular spray fountains cool the water by spraying it into the air. Inside the climate-controlled building, one can gauge the outdoor temperature by the height of the rectangular spray, which disappears entirely in winter.

The lakes form a sophisticated landscape composition. At the entry to the site, the larger, lower lake and spray fountains create a glorious presentation of the Administration Building. From inside the building, the two lakes appear almost equal in size. Without the lower lake, the upper lake with its island and picturesque willows and Henry Moore sculpture would look too precious. As it is, Henry Moore's *Hill Arches* is much more at home here than the Moores attempting to jolly up empty urban plazas across the country,[13] but its smooth mass isn't about anything in particular, which is in keeping with the pastoral mode. Deere's landscape would be more modern and have deeper resonance if its sculpture were to address icono-

graphically or metaphorically the meaning of Deere & Company. Beyond *Hill Arches,* the rectangular spray fountains are a tantalizing hint of the potential beauty of a design that addresses the modern agricultural landscape, especially when seen against the romantic pastoral landscape. The utilitarian fountains are an obvious reminder of agricultural irrigation, and viewed from the side, they remind one of Deere's plows or harrows churning the smooth farm fields.

Dawson's original plan confined the lawn to the area around the upper lake and the building. In Moline's harsh climate, there was no imperative to develop an extensive path system, and Dawson preferred that employees discover their own paths through the woods. Underneath Sasaki's spreading trees, sedge, Solomon's seal, and nightshade would naturalize on the forest floor. These would help retain moisture and would compete for nutrients less than would lawn grass. But in the end, all these arguments counted for less than Deere & Company's new home lawn mower, their first entry in the lawn and garden market. As a demonstration to visiting sales representatives, Deere began to mow everywhere. Since Dawson had wanted a continuous forest canopy to create the low ground cover, he had not used clumps of trees and open meadows in the English landscape style, and with all the mowing, the grounds look more like a golf course than a native Illinois woodland.

Though he regrets the hegemony of the lawn mower, Dawson has nothing but praise for Deere's commitment to the landscape. Dawson or other representatives of Sasaki Associates visit Deere annually to correct problems, consult on new roads and services, and adjust the plantings. Because of the poor porosity of the soils—a problem compounded when construction altered existing drainage patterns—some trees have been moved as many as three times.

An irony of the aesthetics of the Deere landscape is that it is as technologically and structurally determined as the building. Yet most visitors believe the landscape is "natural," that the landscape architect merely cleaned it up a bit and planted some trees along the entry drive. Evidence of technology is repressed in the landscape and celebrated in the building: the machine in the garden.

Over the years, Sasaki Associates' stewardship has focused on the preservation and enhancement of the original design, with a few exceptions—one of the most notable being the addition of a Japanese garden. After the building opened, William Hewitt fell in love with Japanese gardens and brought back five large stones from Kyoto. Instead of creating a private retreat in the woods, Hewitt wanted the stones right next to the building, where he could see them every day. He also insisted on a traditional design—though, of course, such a garden is traditional only in Japan.[14] Hewitt's intuitive response to Japanese gardening was felicitous, since Saarinen's architecture was so strongly influenced by Japanese teahouses and Katsura Palace. But there was no attempt to follow Saarinen's lead and adapt Japanese principles to the scale of the American Midwest and the technology and character of Deere & Company.

Landscape architect Peter Walker once described his profession as that of a "soldier battling without an I-Beam. The architect achieves objectiveness automatically through structure and materials. The landscape architects must consciously strive for objectiveness or their work will become invisible. Too much contemporary landscape architecture is functional and, at best, beautiful, but not meaningful."[15] It falls short of achieving Saarinen's goal: "a total surrounding of permanence, beauty, and meaningfulness . . . of our time and culture."[16]

PROJECT: **DEERE & COMPANY ADMINISTRATION BUILDING**

CLIENT: **DEERE & COMPANY**

DATE OF COMPLETION: **1964**

LOCATION: **MOLINE, ILLINOIS**

ARCHITECTS: **EERO SAARINEN ASSOCIATES, INC.**
PRINCIPAL ASSOCIATE: **KEVIN ROCHE**

LANDSCAPE ARCHITECT: **SASAKI ASSOCIATES, INC.**
PARTNER-IN-CHARGE: **STUART O. DAWSON**

GENERAL CONTRACTOR: **HUBER, HUNT AND NICHOLS**

STRUCTURAL ENGINEER: **ARMANN AND WHITNEY**

LANDSCAPE CONTRACTORS: **DAVEY TREE COMPANY AND LANKENAU-DAMGAARD**

WEYERHAEUSER

TACOMA
WASHINGTON

Comparisons between the Weyerhaeuser Company Headquarters near Tacoma, Washington, and Deere & Company Headquarters are inevitable, since both are major corporate headquarters built across valleys and are landscapes of corporate power and prestige—Weyerhaeuser planted over 2,500 trees, created a large lake, and introduced a sweeping wildflower meadow. Like Deere, Weyerhaeuser illustrates the potential transformation of the pastoral tradition and the inventions of modern landscape architecture. Yet there are critical differences in the two companies' responses to traditional office systems, to regional and corporate identity, and to the pastoral landscape mode.

The Weyerhaeuser Company moved from downtown Tacoma when it was expanding its sales of lumber and other wood products into the international arena. Its new headquarters, a dramatic icon for commuters between Tacoma and Seattle, became a symbol and lightning rod for the company's progressive organization and management. For employees, Weyerhaeuser's most radical innovation was its adoption of an open office landscape or *burolandschaft*: a German office management concept that abolishes partitions, permanent corridors, and almost all private offices. Some of Weyerhaeuser's older officers, tied to traditional corporate hierarchies, left the company. But, encouraged by the president's cautiously inclusive management style—his own office is simply an open desk on the fifth floor—the majority of employees embraced the new spirit. One explained: " 'Open landscape' is not a goldfish bowl as much as it provides access. It's easy to grab someone if you don't have to knock on their door. Some people

View of the meadow and woods from inside the building.

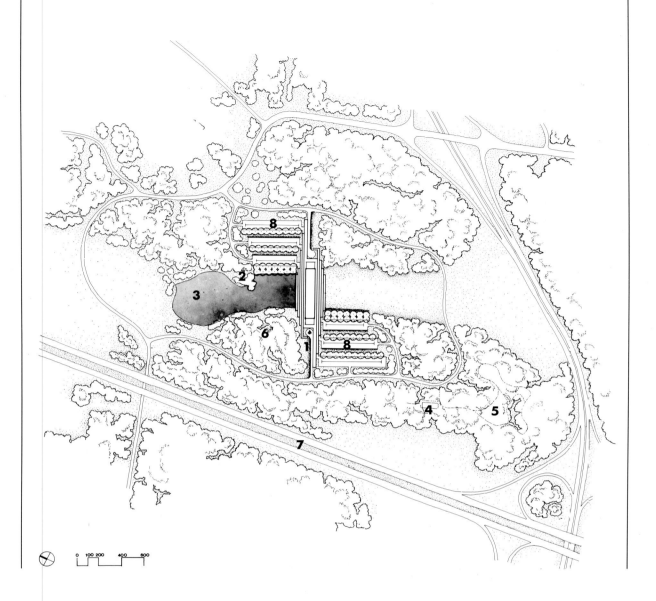

don't like it, but the management has been very committed to it."[1]

The boldness of Weyerhaeuser's planning and design, as well as its northwestern sensibility, owes much to George Weyerhaeuser, the great grandson of the company's founder, who became president and CEO in 1966. Before he assumed the position, the company had commissioned a design by architect Gordon Bunshaft of Skidmore, Owings & Merrill's New York office; that building was to be a dramatic celebration of wood with laminated beams over seventeen feet deep. But Bunshaft's site plan was inwardly focused and this disturbed Weyerhaeuser, who wanted the new headquarters to project a civic presence that would be visible from the nearby interstate highway. Since Weyerhaeuser was also uncomfortable with the theatricality of Bunshaft's design, he decided to replace him with E. Charles (Chuck) Bassett (1921–) of Skidmore, Owings & Merrill's San Francisco office.

The lead landscape architect, Peter Walker (1932–) of Sasaki, Walker and Associates, was born and raised in San Francisco and recognized the clash of regional personalities. "George Weyerhaeuser was a forester. A simple, very direct northwesterner. Bunshaft was a New Yorker who had a fabulous collection of modern art. Chuck Bassett collected crafts, which George admired.

Chuck understood that George wanted refinement and simplicity, but not ostentation."[2]

Although he loved wood and had naturally assumed that the building would be constructed primarily of wood, Weyerhaeuser also wanted a durable and economically sound building, which is why one of the world's leading lumber producers has a concrete-clad headquarters today. The raked exposed aggregate finish blends into the rugged northwestern landscape, and its rough texture sets off the refinement of the wood details and finishes inside.

Walker had been the landscape architect for Foothill College, a highly acclaimed campus near Palo Alto, California. Weyerhaeuser's first idea was to emulate Foothill's cluster of low wooden buildings, but it was unwieldy to disperse the company's 900 employees in a series of small compounds. The existing site was a gentle valley between Interstate 5 and a state freeway and was in a semi-derelict state from random occupation and industrial use. Walker's first conceptual plans for Weyerhaeuser showed the building stepping down the sides of the valley, but in the absence of strong landscape features and the difficulty of locating all the required parking on one side of the valley, Walker and Bassett decided to span the valley and divide the parking on either side. Once Weyerhaeuser embraced the *burolandschaft* concept, spanning the valley allowed Bassett to keep the building compact with extravagantly deep floor plans.

The circulation is as logical and efficient as a mathematical theorem. Beginning with a very deep office space on the floor of the valley, the architects progressively narrowed and shortened the four upper floors so that the building assumed the mass of an earthen dam. The middle section of the valley was cleared to open the building to both highways. Both visitors and employees may arrive at either end of the building. The employee parking lots are terraced down the hillside so employees can enter directly onto their level. Visitors park under long concrete canopies—topped by lush ivy—that project from the building. Below the canopies, on the side away from the parking lots, grass terraces

gracefully pinwheel off and meet the woods. The building uses a quincunx grid, which encourages the *burolandschaft* by avoiding rows of columns. The grid also allows long, unobstructed views of a wildflower meadow on the south side and a ten-acre lake to the north through one of the longest mullionless glass walls in the world. The landscape of nature and the landscape of the office open themselves to each other.

In a similar setting at Deere & Company Headquarters, the architecture is a bridge built on the land. At Weyerhaeuser, the landscape visually crosses the building with the wide bands of ivy on each floor and the green patina of the copper roof. What had been for motorists an indifferent view across the valley was vivified by the insertion of the building's glaucous expanse and Weyerhaeuser's special variance from the Department of Transportation for a more open highway barrier permitting an unobstructed view of the building from Interstate 5.

Weyerhaeuser's landscape favors frankness of form over delightful detailing and picturesque compositions. Peter Walker considers it "more forest management than landscape design." For example, the wildflower meadow was shaped so that parts would be wetter, creating a more random floriferous pattern. Walker planted drifts of alders as highlights against the dark Douglas firs, even though "Weyerhaeuser hated alders. To foresters, they're trash trees. Every time I saw him he would ask if I was planting any more alders."[3]

Weyerhaeuser's landscape design is a celebration of the theme of human order and natural order. The parking lots, instead of being hidden away from the building, are highlighted by rows of London plane trees and carefully trimmed banks of ivy. From above, the cars might be flowers in a Brobdingnagian parterre garden. But the parking projects only on one side, while the woods come up the bank below the visitors' parking on the other. These countervailing elements in the site plan theatricalize the treaty negotiated between commerce and nature.

The site plan is a completely open figure. Not only are the highways unscreened, but there are no clumps of trees, sculpture, or other scale ref-

The long bands of ivy make the landscape appear to flow across the Weyerhaeuser building. This lake view is dominated by the 120-foot flagpole, which is made of laminated wood weighing almost five tons. The flag measures thirty-five feet by fifty feet. OVERLEAF

erence in the middle ground between the building and the end of the valley. This frank acknowledgment of the building and its necessary landscape elements, such as the parking lots, is immanently modern, but as a result the site suffers from a lack of any kind of particularization tying it firmly to Weyerhaeuser. Had Peter Walker *truly* been practicing forest management (as it is known to Weyerhaeuser Company), he might have used fir tree plantations to order the site or, if he had been practicing ecological forest management, he might have used alders and birches as natural colonizers and allowed for natural succession instead of planting them in pictorial fashion at the edge of the woods. Instead, Walker responded to the openness

and straightforwardness of the architecture by avoiding pastoral landscape conventions. The lake at Weyerhaeuser looks unfinished because it violates most of the cardinal rules of pastoral landscape design. For one, it doesn't wrap around a peninsula or island so that we might imagine it to be larger. Nor are there trees in the foreground, as there are at Deere, to give the lake perspective depth. The Weyerhaeuser lake was formed by diverting a shallow creek to an underground channel beneath the building; the water then filled to the existing contours, where it was stabilized. This process replicates vernacular agricultural ponds, but Walker was doing nothing more than holding true to the logic of the construction.

Guardian Rock stands vigil at the main entrance. When sculptor Gordon Newell found the rock, it was in two pieces, probably split by an earthquake.

Sidewalks lined with London plane trees lead from each level of the parking lots so that employees can walk directly onto their respective floors.

The only rhetorical gesture that violates Walker's concept is the huge fifty-foot by thirty-five-foot American flag at the far edge of the parking lot, where it dominates the lake. The rest of the "art" at Weyerhaeuser takes more from nature than from artifice.

The main entrance is marked by the seventy-ton *Guardian Rock*, selected by sculptor Gordon Newell. Its transportation and installation cost as much as a Henry Moore, especially after a small pipe was drilled through the rock's center so seeping water would encourage moss to grow—though the pipe broke a couple of times and was finally abandoned. Even with the moss, the backdrop of rugged, raked concrete subdued the megalith, rendering it more domestic than druidic.

More fortuitous was the resolution of the executive roof garden. Danny Powell, Sasaki, Walker and Associates' principal in charge of field supervision, one day found himself unexpectedly talking with George Weyerhaeuser. Powell, another native northwesterner, discovered that he and Weyerhaeuser shared a passion for rhododendrons. Sensing a kindred spirit, Weyerhaeuser asked Powell's

A drift of birches at the edge of the meadow sets off the massive forest of mature fir trees behind.

opinion of Walker's proposed executive roof garden: an abstraction of a Japanese rock garden. Powell replied that he did not understand why a tree-growing company would have an inanimate garden at its ceremonial center. "That is exactly what has been bothering me," exclaimed Weyerhaeuser, "I just couldn't put my finger on it. You go back and tell Pete Walker to fix it." Powell, who had been with Sasaki, Walker and Associates for less than a year, thought this might result in his looking for another job, but instead Walker told him to find something Weyerhaeuser would like.[4]

After a long search, Powell located a magnificent cut-leaf Japanese maple (*Acer palmatum dissectum* "Atropurpureum") that had been featured at the 1915 Panama Pacific Exhibition in San Francisco and subsequently removed to a nursery. Carefully transplanted with a temporary windscreen, the more-than-century-old tree now flourishes in its place of honor on Weyerhaeuser's roof.

In the larger landscape, Powell worked hard to regenerate the derelict site, using masses of trees of varying sizes to "fill in the gaps." Over 2,500 trees were planted (Weyerhaeuser knows how to plant a forest!), and except for those in the parking lot and the bright drifts of alders and birches, they were used to cover construction scars or to amplify existing plantings. Despite the apparent fecundity of the surrounding woods, the valley actually sup-

ports a fairly narrow range of vegetation. Much of the soil is glacial till, with three- or four-inch stones. When disturbed, it tends either to hold too much water or to turn into quicksand; laborers planting the plane trees in the parking lots often sank into the ground. Sasaki, Walker and Associates used as many as three drain pipes per tree to keep the moisture level down. Weeping willows, one of the hardiest water-loving trees, could not survive the saturated soils around the lake, nor have any of the substitutes done well.

It was not easy to convince Weyerhaeuser to plant two thousand trees that no one would notice, Chuck Bassett remembers. "The site was a mess. It was a cut-over forest on the urban fringe, all cut up by country roads with abandoned shacks and houses. [Weyerhaeuser officials] didn't understand why it was necessary to clean it up. We had a hard time getting them to realize how important it was for the concept of the landscape. . . . Eventually they really started looking after the place."[5]

Since the headquarters opened, Weyerhaeuser's stewardship has been exemplary, and the company has continued to develop new programs without compromising the original design. Sasaki, Walker and Associates later helped build a forty-acre rhododendron garden whose lanky informality was recently complemented by the Pacific Rim Bonsai Collection, an addition that is at once ironic and

The small John Shethar Memorial Garden is an intimate retreat overlooking the lake.

An eastern larch grown by bonsai artist Nick Lenz. It represents the Christian who grows away from God in his youth, winds back in midlife, and grows toward the center as he reaches old age. It is estimated to be about 160 years old.

Another sensitive addition was the John Shethar Memorial Garden, designed by William Callaway of the SWA Group (the firm that evolved from Sasaki, Walker and Associates). Callaway folded the garden into the hillside overlooking the pond, where it would not be visible from the building. It is a small, carefully crafted garden designed for intimate retreats or contemplation. A flagstone terrace is cut into the hillside, and water bubbles up from what might be a spring were it not for the telltale drill marks. The water then drips from a small stone cavity in the hillside and runs between the straight line of the terrace and the jagged rock ledge. A single Douglas fir punctuates the taut surface of the flagstone plane.

This is as close to romance as one comes at Weyerhaeuser. Mt. Rainier is visible from the upper level, but the building makes no acknowledgment of it. Instead of trying to rise above the manifestos of modernism, the designers dug in deeper until only the essential landscape and elemental building remained.

apposite, especially since the climate is perfectly tailored to the art of bonsai. Both collections are highly regarded and many a connoisseur comes to visit them throughout the year.

PROJECT: **WEYERHAEUSER INTERNATIONAL HEADQUARTERS**

CLIENT: **WEYERHAEUSER COMPANY**

DATE OF COMPLETION: **1971**

LOCATION: **TACOMA, WASHINGTON**

ARCHITECTS: **SKIDMORE, OWINGS & MERRILL**
PRINCIPAL-IN-CHARGE: **E. CHARLES BASSETT**

LANDSCAPE ARCHITECTS: **SASAKI, WALKER AND ASSOCIATES**
PARTNER-IN-CHARGE: **PETER WALKER**

ROOF GARDEN: LANDSCAPE ARCHITECT: **RICHARD A. VIGNOLO**

SHETHAR MEMORIAL GARDEN: LANDSCAPE ARCHITECT:
WILLIAM CALLAWAY, THE SWA GROUP

PACIFIC RIM BONSAI COLLECTION: LANDSCAPE ARCHITECT:
THOMAS L. BERGER ASSOCIATES, P.S.

SPACE PLANNERS: **SIDNEY RODGERS ASSOCIATES**

GENERAL CONTRACTOR: **SWINERTON AND WALBERG**

LANDSCAPE CONTRACTOR: **LANDSCAPING, INC.**

THE BLOEDEL RESERVE

S E A T T L E
W A S H I N G T O N

When Prentice and Virginia Bloedel decided to dedicate their property to future public use, they chose to call the 160-acre site on Bainbridge Island, near Seattle, the Bloedel *Reserve,* because a reserve is a tract of land set aside for a special purpose. Bloedel came to define that purpose after living on the property for more than thirty years and after hiring a succession of landscape architects, ecologists, horticulturalists, and other specialists to help shape his vision of a place where "one feels the existence of a divine order. Man is not set apart from the rest of nature—he is just a member of that incredibly diverse population of the universe, a member that nature can do without, but who cannot do without nature."[1] Bloedel's sentiments are spiritually descended from the nineteenth-century American transcendentalists such as Ralph Waldo Emerson, who wrote in *Nature* (1836) that the terms "God" and "nature" could be used interchangeably, and from William Wordsworth, Jean Jacques Rousseau, and other romantic poets and philosophers. Bloedel's vision also embraced some Oriental attitudes toward nature, but with the caveat that the Reserve should "find an expression of this philosophical dimension, indigenous and appropriate to this country. . . . In other words, we would like to capture the essence of the Japanese garden—the qualities of naturalness, subtlety, reverence, tranquillity—and construct a Western expression of it."[2]

Celebrating growth, decay, and regeneration, the Reserve uses the complementary forces of yin

The open meadow behind the bird marsh provides additional habitats for birds.

and yang to create a harmonious whole. Its design embraces Western garden traditions, the "constructed nature" found in Japanese gardens, and the self-renewing processes of the land itself. While the Reserve is infused with older romantic attitudes toward nature, its artful expression is firmly rooted in the twentieth century. This rich layering of history and reclamation, of nature and artifice, has produced a providential unity that, in Prentice Bloedel's words, "breaks the connection with the outside world, conditions the mind, [and] stirs feelings akin to those of our less sophisticated forebears."[3]

The Reserve is now managed by the Arbor Fund,[4] a nonprofit foundation established to assure perpetual maintenance, but from 1951 to 1987 it was the private residence of the Bloedel family. The main house straddles the two complementary hemispheres of the Reserve's design. To the north is a series of landscape compositions and habitats, including three lakes bordered by immaculate lawns, a rhododendron glen, an orchid walk, a moss garden, and a Japanese garden. Balancing these idealized landscapes is the recently opened south forest, where natural succession is allowed to run its course. Spiritually and physically bridging the two hemispheres is the bird marsh, a carefully constructed "natural" habit. There, each spring brings, in landscape architect Richard Haag's description, "a reaffirmation of the lifetides with all kinds of birds squawking, courting, and mating."[5]

This ambitious vision of the Reserve was not what the Bloedels had in mind when they purchased the property in 1950. They were simply looking for a house and admired the understated French Revival

Sunlit leaves of a Japanese maple.

style of the main house (1931), which is situated on a promontory with a commanding view of Puget Sound.

Because the property had been completely logged early in the century, much of it was overgrown and could only be explored with a machete. Prentice Bloedel was then vice-chairman of his family's lumber company, one of the largest in British Columbia, and had developed a deep sense of responsibility and love for the land and its resources. He soon began exploring his property's old logging roads and "discovered that there is grandeur in decay: the rotten log hosting seedlings of hemlocks, cedars, huckleberries, the shape of a crumbling snag."[6] Even today, both of the Reserve's hemispheres retain memories of the original Douglas firs and hemlocks in the form of giant stumps with ominous "logging eyes"—holes punched into the lower trunks to support platforms for the loggers as they sawed away the upper timbers. Because the bases of the giant trees were too irregular to be of commercial value, they were left to sprout volunteers and became covered with ferns, lichens, and huckleberries. It was not easy for Bloedel to

The mound behind the Japanese sand and rock garden by Dr. Koichi Kawana was originally planted with blue fescue to harmonize with the blue atlas cedar (right), but in the Reserve's moist topography the fescue was blue only during the summer months, so it was replaced with dwarf cotoneaster for uniform color and less weeding.

The moss garden's serpentine path winds among the moss-covered alders and red cedar stumps.

appreciate those ghosts of the grandeur of the virgin forest because, as he admitted, years of family involvement with the timber industry did not cultivate an appreciation of stumps.[7] Nor was it easy for him to admire the special beauty and utility of the Reserve's alders—which are considered a weed tree by most lumbermen.[8] Although Bloedel never apologized for his timber baron ancestors, his own explorations of the property moved him beyond the ethical and moral compass of good stewardship toward a more romantic and mystical relationship with the land.

The chronology of the Reserve's different designers reflects the Bloedels' evolution from an early desire for domestic comfort, through the slow maturation of their mystical vision, to the assumption of responsibility for sharing that vision with the public. Intrigued by the site's potential, but with no training in design, Bloedel called on many different landscape architects, gardeners, scientists, horticulturalists, and engineers. He eventually accumulated an impressive archive of "unbuilt," "revised" or "later removed" designs. The designers were not commissioned to work on one project at a time and most of the areas of the Reserve received input from different professionals over the years, so there is no area of the Reserve that can be credited in its entirety to a single designer, nor is the chronology of the Reserve's development easy to trace.

The Bloedels first employed landscape designer Otto Holmdahl, a Swede who had worked for Virginia Bloedel's mother. However, they soon found him "too set in his ways"[9] and in 1954 they turned to Tommy Church. During his twenty-year intermittent association with the Bloedels, Church generated a number of different designs. Some of the earlier ones included a five-hole golf course, tennis courts, a swimming pool, and the siting of a guest house, but few of Church's designs were ever realized or survived past the 1960s.

Church did make several lasting contributions, however, including the orchid walk between the north loop road and the guest house. Here native coral root orchids (Corallorhiza maculata) were planted under a dense stand of fir trees so that the low light levels and fallen needles would prevent other ground cover from competing with the orchids. It is an especially magical prelude to the openness of the north meadow. Church's most significant design was the 200-foot-long rectangular reflection pond. Listening to Bloedel speak of his love of European canals, Church noted that the water table was less than a foot below the surface and suggested that a serene pool could be formed simply by placing a concrete curb in the wet ground, excavating a few feet, and letting the ground water fill the area from the bottom.

The Bloedels were not satisfied with Church's plan to allow the woods to grow to the edge of the pool. They were more sympathetic to a later suggestion by landscape architect Richard Haag to enclose the pool with a series of ten-foot-tall pruned English yew hedges (Taxus baccata "Fastigiata") that would transform the place from a reflection "pond" into a reflection "garden." Because yews have an aversion to "wet feet," it is a tribute to the Reserve's diligent and determined maintenance that the hedge has retained most of its fullness and solidity. For the pond's perimeter, Prentice Bloedel designed curved benches out of old wooden trusses

from a Bainbridge Island shipyard.

In its final form, the reflection garden is remarkably similar to a well-known section of Courances, a formal French garden near Paris, first designed by André Le Nôtre in the seventeenth century and later revised and reconstructed by Achille Duchêne (1866–1947) in the early twentieth century. The pond at Courances is much longer— over 1,800 feet—but has the same arrangement of overlapping hedges that hide the entrance when one is inside. The dialogue between tradition and invention accounts for the subtle differences between the pond at Courances and the reflection garden. At Courances, an evenly spaced row of tall poplars is visible beyond the frame of the boxwood hedge, while the Reserve's yew hedge is much higher, so the trunks of the surrounding trees are shielded from the interior views, and one sees only the straight line of the hedges, the seemingly airborne branches, and the sky. In the water's reflection, the sky evokes John Constable's dictum that clouds are the chief organ of sentiment in landscape painting.

During the mid-1950s, when there was a surge of regional interest in residential Japanese gardens, the Bloedels commissioned Fujitaro Kubota, a native of Japan who had been designing Japanese gardens in the northwest since 1923, to design a Japanese stroll garden below the guest house. Kubota convinced the Bloedels to refill part of the newly excavated swan lake and create a separate pond for the Japanese garden.

The garden, in deference to Mr. Bloedel's instructions not to create a stereotypical Japanese garden, had no lacquered bridges, stone lanterns, or shrines, but its key plantings of pines, cypresses, and maples were pruned in classical Japanese style. During the 1960s, perhaps due to disinterest or the Bloedels' discomfort with the strong Japanese look of the garden, the plantings were not maintained.[10] In the late 1970s, landscape architect Richard Yamasaki was hired by the Reserve to improve the paths and restore some of the plantings. Today the Reserve tries to maintain the plantings so they will appear more "natural" than those in an authentic Japanese garden.

In the mid-1970s, as Bloedel entered his

A solitary bench, chosen by Virginia Bloedel, looks out over the bird marsh.

The reflection garden. The benches were designed by Prentice Bloedel out of wooden trusses from a nearby shipyard. OVERLEAF

seventies, his concerns turned from the domestic designs of Church and Kubota to "the psychological, philosophical and anthropological aspects of aesthetics . . . the components of nature that effect the most elevating and enduring pleasure for man."[11] In 1978 he commissioned Richard Haag, who brought an introspection and a desire "to arouse latent emotional and aesthetic instincts and feelings, and to reaffirm man's immutable and timeless bond with nature. . . ."[12]

Haag had been strongly influenced by two years of study and travel in Japan in the mid-1950s, and his approach to design has more to do with an Eastern "nonstriving" sensibility than with Western architectural practice. He begins by working with clients or constituencies to get them to "buy into a vision before I show them any plans," a process too time-consuming for more normative professional offices. Haag's emotional investment in the project meant spending many hours with Bloedel and the Reserve's director, Richard Brown, slowly consulting the *genius loci*. Like every other designer who worked for the Bloedels, Haag found many of his ideas revised or discarded, but he still felt an instinctive bond with Bloedel, calling him a "well-centered man of great sensitivity and vision." Haag loved walking the site with its owner, who was slightly lame from childhood polio and would use his heavy walking stick to urge Haag to see the calligraphy of the mosses and lichens.[13]

Among Haag's first projects for the Reserve were the completion of the reflection garden, a

Paul Kirk's guest house overlooks the Japanese stroll garden designed by Fujitaro Kubota.

The many evergreens in the Japanese garden create a rich tapestry of different textures and subtle gradations of green.

redesign of the entry road, and the resolution of the east bluff, which separates the main house from the lower plateau. The bluff, which had always been visually ragged, was regraded into a clearly defined trapezoidal wedge of St.-John's-wort (*Hypericum*), an evergreen ground cover with bright yellow flowers during the summer months that is widely used as ground cover for eroded highway embankments. The St.-John's-wort ends at the base of the bluff, where it meets the flowing lines of a grassy meadow bordered by large mounds and tree plantings that lead the eye toward a clump of fir trees and Puget Sound. A path at the end of the grassy meadow connects the north and south hemispheres of the Reserve and allows visitors to view both the sound and the dramatic wedge of St.-John's-wort.[14]

Later, Haag's energies were directed toward

an irrigation pond that needed to be enlarged. Haag suggested creating a bird marsh as part of the necessary enlargements. Working with ornithologists, who helped devise a matrix of plants and different nesting habitats, Haag removed some adjoining trees to give herons and other waterfowl a "longer flight path" and dug a new pond next to the existing one, complete with seven nesting islands. His original plan to carve fingers of water reaching into the deep woods was stymied when the bulldozers bogged down in heavy fall rains. The pond quickly filled up, a sure sign that nature had completed the work of art.

For Haag and the Bloedels, recognizing nature's role did not rule out an appropriate formal response. The constructed naturalness of the bird marsh complements the geometrical rigor of the reflection pond, a restatement of the Reserve's yin-yang theme.

While the bird marsh was being dredged, Haag began working on the north side of the guest house—designed in the early 1960s by architect Paul Hayden Kirk. The house, which combined elements of Japanese architecture, Northwest Indian long houses, and modern skylights, overlooked the Japanese garden to the south. The north side had a swimming pool, which the Bloedels wanted removed, and lacked any spatial definition. Haag addressed the latter problem by constructing a series of mounds between the pool and the north meadow. They were planted in different ground covers and ranged in diameter from forty feet to one hundred feet. In place of the swimming pool, Haag proposed to build two pyramids of moss, one upright and the other inverted. The concrete pool apron was sawed into an irregular checkerboard pattern of grass and concrete squares, which would appear to revolve around the planned pyramids

View of the trapezoidal wedge of St.-John's-wort and Puget Sound from the rear terrace of the main house.

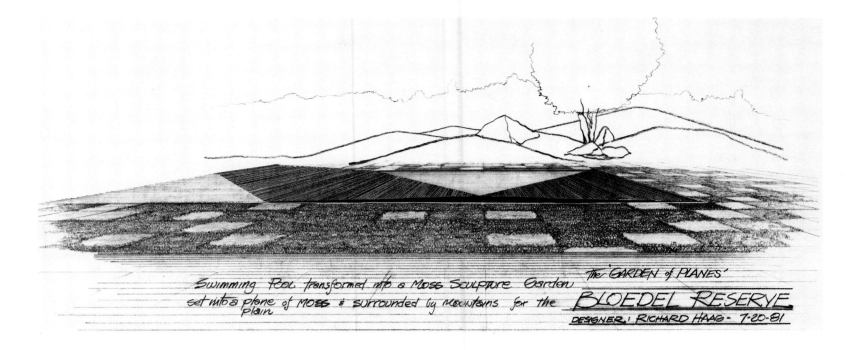

Swimming Pool transformed into a Moss Sculpture Garden The 'GARDEN of PLANES'
set into a plane of MOSS & surrounded by mountains for the **BLOEDEL RESERVE**
DESIGNER: RICHARD HAAG · 7·20·81

Richard Haag's sketch of the Garden of Planes, which was replaced by Dr. Koichi Kawana's traditional Japanese sand and rock garden. Courtesy of Rich Haag.

The large rock next to the Japanese sand and rock garden is surrounded by *Bolax glebaria*, a tufted evergreen perennial from the Falkland Islands. The square pavers are the remains of the old swimming pool deck.

and slide under the enclosing mounds. Haag called this soft, mysterious composition the "Garden of Planes," and described it as a "Buddhist garden of mindfulness" whose enigmatic qualities would stimulate reflection in the manner of the Zen gardens of Japan.[15]

Bloedel had reservations but agreed to the construction of a preliminary mock-up using crushed gravel instead of moss because the Bloedels thought it would take too long for the moss to cover the mock-up. The gravel made an austere white sculpture that remained in place for about three years until Bloedel and the board of the Arbor Fund decided the Garden of Planes was "too artificial" and contrary to the spirit of the Reserve and had it removed. Its successor, designed by Dr. Koichi Kawana, a professor of landscape architecture at UCLA, is a traditional Zen sand and rock garden similar to the famous Ryoan-ji near Kyoto. Haag's moss pyramids visually "called" to the mounds and thus extended the perceptual space of the small Garden of Planes to the larger landscape. The present stone garden needs the kind of wall that encloses all similar gardens in Japan so that one is not visually distracted by the scale changes between the small stones, the large mounds, and the expansive meadow beyond. But more importantly, it betrays a lack of confidence by *building the past* instead of *building on the past,* as the reflection garden and other areas of the Reserve do so confidently.

Visitors had to walk through a damp amorphous space between the guest house and the reflection pond and Bloedel solicited solutions from many different designers. The idea of a moss garden began to emerge when Richard Haag and Richard Brown saw a moss carpet in a small part of the Nitobe Botanical Garden in Vancouver. Around the same time, Bloedel's daughter and her husband returned from Japan with pictures of Saiho-ji in Kyoto, known as the "Moss Temple." Originally created by a Zen priest in the fourteenth century, Saiho-ji's complex of small buildings and its stroll garden gradually fell into ruin and were consumed by moss.

Haag used what he called "selective subtrac-

tions of the nuances of nature from the chaos of a tangled bog." The area was cleared of underbrush and Richard Brown suggested planting over 275,000 starts of Irish moss (which is not a true moss) for the mosses to grow over. The mosses thrived and eventually covered the old stumps left from the first logging operation. Bloedel was taken with the primeval quality of the moss-covered floor and suggested building on that aspect with a dense planting of Devil's Walking Stick (*Aralia spinosa*)—a coarse plant with long bright green leaves, clubby stems, and dangerous thorny spines (which help prevent visitors from straying off the path onto the delicate moss). Together with the ferns and huckleberries, the aralia enacts a primordial drama. Haag called the moss garden a "garden of extraction where the aroma, the heavy smells of death and decay seep into your mind."[16]

The Zen priest who created Saiho-ji wrote of the original garden, perhaps with a premonition of its surrender to moss, "It is delusion to think that the pure world of paradise and the profane world of the present are different. The distinction between holy purity and defilement, too, is delusion." This philosophy resonates at the Reserve in the fulfillment of Prentice Bloedel's wish to "look to the Orient for inspiration and adapt it to enrich our own culture."[17] The purity of the moss covers the decaying remains of the virgin forest that was so profanely harvested. At the reflection pond, we see the harvested timber serving as benches.[18] The formal hedge inscribes a pure, abstract line against the slow growth of the moss garden—the latter is "letting go" while the former is carefully maintained.

Both the hedge and the moss garden, like most of the idealized landscapes in the northern hemisphere of the Reserve, require Sisyphean maintenance to achieve the illusion of naturalness. For example, the small "Christmas pond" in the rhododendron glen continually fills with silt. Large mud pumps and a clam-shell dredge have been used to clean it and the muck periodically has to be cleaned out by hand with three-gallon buckets. Similarly, the lawn edge of the large pond at the center of the property is shaped by bags of concrete mix, drains, and filter fabric. And the sod must be

The Reserve has an extensive primrose collection. Featured here are candelabra primroses (*Primula pulverulenta*) and behind them, yellow iris (*Iris pseudacorus*).

replaced every year because there is not enough soil to sustain a healthy lawn.

These problems, heightened all the more by the prospect of opening the Reserve to the public in 1989, convinced Bloedel and the Arbor Fund that a more pragmatic approach was needed and in 1985 they engaged the services of Environmental Planning & Design (EPD), a landscape architecture firm based in Pittsburgh. Haag's relationship with the Reserve, already strained by the controversy over his Garden of Planes and by the necessity of reporting to the Arbor Fund board instead of directly to Bloedel and Brown, was terminated.[19]

EPD had designed many important botanical gardens and arboretums, including the Chicago Botanic Gardens, and was commissioned to "organize the Reserve in accordance with Bloedel's criteria and sensitivity."[20] Specifically, EPD was asked to refine certain areas, develop long-term maintenance strategies, integrate the south forest into the trail system, and design the parking and visitor facilities. Geoffrey Rausch, EPD's partner-

in-charge, has taken great pains to understand Bloedel's vision and, as Bloedel's involvement in the daily operations steadily diminishes,[21] to insure that this vision endures in the planning and maintenance. "It's been a hell of an education for me," Rausch has remarked. "One thing I learned very quickly is that the Bloedels loved the land and understood it better than anyone else."[22]

A significant problem EPD addressed was orchestrating visitor circulation. Since the development of the Reserve had been guided by Bloedel's evolving vision and not by a coherent master plan, there was no entirely satisfactory way to lead visitors through the site. Rausch's solution was for visitors to park near the entrance to the property, walk across the meadow to the bird marsh, then proceed through the less managed south forest, emerging near the central lakes, and walk to the main house—now converted into a visitor's information center. After this pause, visitors walk down through the rhododendron glen and along the Orchid Walk to the guest house and Japanese

The tranquil beauty of the bench and overhanging cherry tree next to the main house attracted the Bloedels when they purchased the property in 1951.

gardens. They then walk through the moss garden and reach the reflection garden, which becomes, in Rausch's words, "man's perfection in nature—the supreme moment of reflection where you can gather all your thoughts before walking back through the meadow to your car."[23]

This route loses the metaphysical connection between the purity of the reflection garden and the fecundity of the bird marsh, but an alternative route, proposed by Haag, was no better in its totality. Haag also suggested parking near the entrance, but then advised proceeding directly to what would have been the Garden of Planes, followed by the moss garden, the reflection garden, and the bird marsh, so that the experience would alternate between the geometrical gardens and those structured by natural processes. Unfortunately, the rest of the tour is somewhat anticimactic, in that the rhododendron glen does not possess enough drama to be the final act of the Reserve's highly theatrical yin-yang experience.

Bloedel's ultimate vision was to offer visitors as solitary a communion with nature as is possible in a public reserve. EPD decided not to provide alternative paths so that there would be no need for directional signs. In most places the paths are narrow to prevent visitors from bunching up along the way. The Arbor Fund now limits the number of visitors to about 150 a day and gives them only a simple guide map at the beginning of the tour to encourage them to experience the Reserve emotionally and spiritually rather than follow a nature guide. More detailed information about the place is available to anyone who wants it at the main house at the mid-point of the visit.

The Reserve continues to evolve gradually through both natural processes and pragmatic responses to Bloedel's vision and to visitors. The deep joy of the Bloedel Reserve is felt microcosmically in the delicacy of the mosses and the vibrant stillness of the bird marsh, and macrocosmically in its dialogue with distant garden traditions, Oriental philosophy, transcendentalism, and Romantic poetry. At the Reserve, the classical dichotomy between man and nature dissolves and, in the words of Virginia Bloedel's favorite poet, William Wordsworth:

While with an eye made quiet by the power
Of harmony, and the deep power of joy,
We see into the life of things.[24]

PROJECT: **THE BLOEDEL RESERVE, 1951—**

CLIENT: **MR. AND MRS. PRENTICE BLOEDEL**

LOCATION: **BAINBRIDGE ISLAND, WASHINGTON**

MANAGEMENT: **THE ARBOR FUND**

DIRECTOR: **RICHARD BROWN**

MASTER PLAN: **ENVIRONMENTAL PLANNING AND DESIGN**
PARTNER-IN-CHARGE: **GEOFFREY RAUSCH**

LANDSCAPE ARCHITECT 1978–85: **RICHARD HAAG AND ASSOCIATES**

PREVIOUS LANDSCAPE ARCHITECT: **THOMAS DOLLIVER CHURCH**

UPPER JAPANESE GARDEN: **DR. KOICHI KAWANA**

LOWER JAPANESE GARDEN: **FUJITARO KUBOTA**

GUEST HOUSE ARCHITECT: **PAUL HAYDEN KIRK**

TWO

MODERN SPACE

In classical gardens, space was always clearly circumscribed; classical designers believed that space could not be perceived in nature and only became perceivable when it was unambiguously bounded by buildings or verdant enclosures. By the twentieth century, however, this concept of space was being challenged by artists, architects, designers, and scientists alike. Albert Einstein rejected the very term "space": "We entirely shun the vague word 'space', of which . . . we cannot form the slightest conception and we replace it with 'motion relative to a practically rigid body of reference.' "[1] Paul Cézanne and other artists dismantled perspectival space in painting, while the futurists argued that the speed of modern transportation and machinery made the classical concept of static space as antiquated as the horse and buggy. In architecture, the ideals of modern space were clearly articulated by Le Corbusier, Frank Lloyd Wright, and Mies Van der Rohe. Their plans provided for an uninterrupted flow of space that could not be captured from a single vantage point. Landscape designers began to look at what they termed "the spatial continuum" in nature. Landscape architect Lawrence Halprin observed that "spaces all move into other spaces and are non-confined."[2] Instead of being static, space flowed freely through the entire world, moving past boundaries and objects, like water flowing downstream. Space became, for many designers, an end in itself, and design students were taught that space was the most important objective of modern design. It was a free, living, breathing thing that designers had to be careful not to "kill" with too many objects or too tight an enclosure.

"Free space" has long had a particularly strong appeal for Americans, whose cultural attitudes toward space were shaped by the always-beckoning frontier. It dominated the American psyche and was celebrated in many paeans to the "open road"—from Walt Whitman to Jack Kerouac. For such adventurers, being within a well-defined space was, in Huckleberry Finn's words, "too sivilized." Motive experience felt more comfortable to Americans and corresponded to democratic ideals of freedom of choice unfettered by political restraints. Enclosed space then became the exception rather than the norm and has often been reserved for sacred or contemplative places.

In England, too, open spaces have been championed since the eighteenth century by such landscape designers as Capability Brown and William Kent. Indeed, English landscape gardens have served as models for many of America's pastoral landscapes, including Olmsted's great urban parks.

Reflecting an awareness of the physical and mental dimensions of space as revealed by modern science, modern landscape designers have tried to create the same dynamic spatial experience that Halprin found in the natural landscape. They have not sought a complete denial of classical space, but an experiential space that is vital and free.

THE WRIGHT HOUSE

When Bagley and Virginia Wright commissioned architect Arthur Erickson (1924–) to design their house on a heavily forested site overlooking Puget Sound, they began by visiting the Bloedel Reserve. Virginia Wright, the daughter of Prentice and Virginia Bloedel, wanted Erickson to see the reflection pond completed by Richard Haag about six years earlier so that Erickson could bring something of the spirit of the Reserve's clearing to their own site. The Wrights knew that Erickson's instinct was to preserve natural features, and the reflection pond suggested a different approach. Bagley Wright, who comes from a family of timber barons, encouraged Erickson with a friendly reminder that "to see the trees you have to cut some of them down."

Erickson realized that not only could the house occupy a clearing in the forest, but that the plan of the house itself could "echo the clearing, with the forest of columns framing the skylit central rooms, [becoming] a simile of the forest clearing."[1] The building and the landscape would construct what was not present on the existing site— bold and factual space. Instead of mimicking the structure of the trees as architect Fay Jones did at the Crosby Arboretum (pages 174–87), Erickson cleared horizontally, realizing that however much he wanted the house's structure to echo the tree trunks, the building could never soar like the eighty-foot-high Douglas firs. Erickson sees all of his architecture as a direct response to a given site: "Architectural language—the horizontal planes and

The house, seen from the daisy-carpeted meadow.

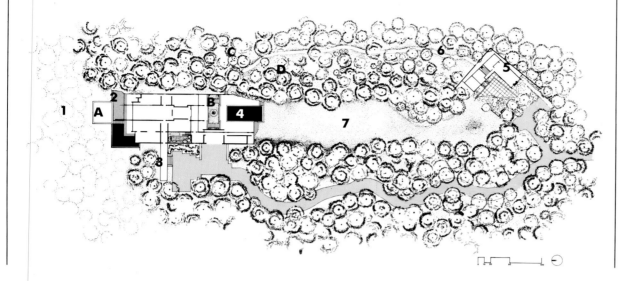

vertical supports that create spatial and structural rhythm—is discovered where the inner requirements of a building meet the external landscape conditions."[2] And he feels that his architecture develops the most direct response to a site when the variety of materials is limited so that the building, together with its surroundings, becomes a sculptural space.

The house is on a nine-acre site in a Seattle residential enclave designed in 1911 by the Olmsted Brothers' landscape architecture firm.[3] The Wrights' landscape architect, Cornelia Hahn Oberlander (1924–   ), extended the Olmsted Brothers' curvilinear road system by carefully designing a winding entrance drive that avoids major trees. Bagley Wright had a six-hundred-foot-long clearing logged, yielding fifty thousand board feet of lumber. This long, irregularly shaped clearing stretches from a dramatic overlook of Puget Sound to a rough termination deep in the woods.

Using a tripartite organization, Erickson created a clearing within the house, centered on a skylit gallery, with the bedrooms, kitchen, and service areas disposed to either side. The central space extends into a wildflower meadow at the east end and, at the west, to the very edge of the steep bank facing Puget Sound. The horizon of the sound was made indeterminate by a still reflecting pool, where water flows imperceptibly over the edge, dematerializing the boundaries of the pool. The viewer looking out at the sound has the illusion of hovering in an indeterminate position between the sky—reflected in the pool—and the sound below. Erickson described the effect of the architecture's extension through the reflection pool and the long meadow: "The building is really just a point of interest on a spatial continuum that extends to the horizon and deep into the forest. The movement has neither beginning nor end. Like a temple drum beat, it fades to infinity."[4]

The house is organized by blocky, H-shaped concrete columns—scaled to human dimensions instead of being a challenge to the scale of the forest. Their shape and placement both inside the house and along the sides of the terraces suggest small Japanese *torii* gates leading into the woods, and at one point they do frame a path through the trees to the guest house. The forest is dark throughout the year, so the red-brown of the trunks and branches form a constant background. One can follow the rhythmic march of the tall, straight fir trees along the forest path. The shadows are so thick that one can see only so far into the woods, where the forest appears as infinite as the sky. If one leaves the path, the soft needled forest floor gives way to thicker underbrush.

The particular quality of light in this region is what Erickson most wanted to capture. "The Northwest Coast is a particularly difficult area with its watery lights, which are capable of sombre and

The edge of the reflecting pool at the back of the house, overlooking Puget Sound.

melancholy moods. The coast demands that buildings . . . permit a gentle introspective light to bathe the walls, or water to reflect the sky's brightness from the earth's dark surfaces."[5]

In most of his work, Erickson has demonstrated a preference for the rough gray of poured-in-place concrete. As he once remarked, "Athenians had their Pentelic marble; we have our concrete."[6] In the clearing of the dark woods, with its soft, hazy light, Erickson needed a warmer tone. Proving that concrete work is a modern craft, he labored with mock-ups and test batches to achieve a wonderful tawny color that lightens the forest edge without overpowering the Wrights' sculpture collection by its contrast. Using golden sand and tinted cement, Erickson had the batches poured every Friday, since the plant mixed regular gray concrete the rest of the week. The concrete's tawny shade is mysteriously soft and laden with its own quiet intensity in the penumbra of the Pacific Northwest.

Despite Erickson's vision of the concrete colonnade as "points on a continuum," it does come to an end because the columns' light color projects against the dark background of the forest, except when rare shafts of bright morning or late afternoon light illuminate the tree trunks. There is a similar contrast between the terrace and the meadow, which is made all the more powerful by the absence of any transitional elements.

The existing clearing had a ten-percent cross slope, and using berms or retaining walls to level it would have undermined the remaining trees (for the terrace, the slope was evened with steps and the caretaker's suite on the lower side). Oberlander's solution was a sculpted meadow designed to disguise the cross slope and create an illusion of greater depth. It begins with a slight declivity at the end of the swimming pool, rises to a few small mounds in the center, then narrows at the far end. It is not level—one side is distinctly higher—but it alleviates a vertiginous view from the terrace. The meadow was seeded with white daisies and just a few other wildflowers because Oberlander prefers solid areas of colors, believing that "the so-called wildflower meadows don't work unless you have a real meadow, not just a small clearing in the forest."[7]

The wildflower meadow was carefully sculpted to disguise the existing steep cross slope.

In the foreground is Anthony Caro's *Warrant* (1971). The planting of hemlocks at the edge of the meadow protects the tall fir trees.

H-shaped concrete columns such as these are the dominant organizational element of the house.

Mark Di Suvero's *Bunjonschess* (1965) looms large in the woods behind the pink azaleas. On the terrace Anthony Caro's *Warrant* (1971) seems to gesture toward the meadow.

This view of the meadow is seen from the entrance drive.
OVERLEAF

The grading of the clearing is deliberately coarse to make it appear that the only intervention was the logging operation and belie Oberlander's on-site modifications. At the edge of the clearing, Oberlander wanted to retain the frame of tall firs with their dark green crowns. Logging out the center of a forest is disruptive and weakens the remaining trees, so Oberlander's solution was to plant small hemlocks—fir trees need direct sunlight while hemlocks will grow in the shade of the towering firs— at the borders of the clearing to protect the exposed firs. In time the hemlocks will grow, and the contrast of the bushy hemlocks against the tall trunks of the firs will disappear. Hemlocks were also used deeper in the woods to thicken the forest and screen views of the highway and neighboring houses. Closer to

the house, rhododendrons, vine maples, and other shrubs were used to knit the house to the ground.

Oberlander and Erickson are long-time collaborators and Oberlander, trained in the modernist tradition of "less is more," credits Erickson with pushing her to broaden her plant palette: "When we were working on Robeson Square [the government center in Vancouver] I used broad sweeps of evergreens, but Arthur said: 'Cornelia, there are many different greens.' And he was right and I started paying much closer attention to subtle variations. Now I'll use different rhododendrons to create a richer tapestry."[8]

In 1987, eight years after the house was completed, the Wrights built a guest house beyond the meadow and visually isolated from the main

Meg Webster's *Conical Depression* in the foreground is another point of interest on the spatial continuum that extends from one end of the site to the other.

Tony Smith's sculptural group *Wandering Rocks* (1967) is situated along the path leading to the guest house. With their sheer, faceted planes and abrupt truncations, these steel solids suggest the basic geometric lines of the house, and their "random" spacing echoes the natural spacing of the fir trees.

residence. Designed by architect John Cutler, it has a complementary relationship to Erickson's design. It is wedged into a small hill and the enclosing concrete walls have an exposed jagged edge that is in sharp contrast to the classical refinement of the main residence.

Bagley and Virginia Wright are passionate art collectors. For them the question was how much the house was to be an armature for their art collection and how much it was to be a work of art itself. But for Erickson, the art of architecture is the creation of space, and space, after all, is what the Wrights needed for their collection. Erickson has asserted that for him "Space is the supreme aesthetic adventure. If meeting the purposes of a building is the major task, making the spaces to celebrate those events is an architect's peculiar delight."[9]

One must be cautious about descriptions of the sculpture collection since the Wrights are constantly adding to, subtracting from, or simply rearranging their collection. Nevertheless, certain themes emerge that give the sculpture a regional resonance that is missing in the collection at PepsiCo. The Wrights' collection ranges across most of the recent movements in modern sculpture, but they have generally placed minimalists indoors—Carl Andre's flat *Zinc-Lead Plain* is another clearing within the main hallway—and proto-minimalists like Tony Smith and Ellsworth Kelly or post-minimalists like Joel Shapiro and Scott Burton outdoors. The outdoor sculptures are not anonymous objects like the Andre piece, but have a lyrical and anecdotal expression that amplifies the human occupation of the clearing. The simultaneous solidity and trans-

The dividing line between the swimming pool and the wildflower meadow is dematerialized by the smooth weir.

parency of Anthony Caro's *Riviera* overlooking the sound is a kind of dance on the skyline, while Joel Shapiro's blocky homunculus flails its arms as it balances precariously on the surface of the reflecting pool. The pieces in the woods have a totemic presence: Mark Di Suvero's *Bunjonschess* is a splayed steel tripod from which three heavy logs dangle—an amusing play on the process of clearing the woods, as well as an improvisational construction made of materials found on the site. More subdued and less interactive is Tony Smith's *Wandering Rocks*—five fragmentary solids inspired by Japanese rock gardens. Their black steel construction has a gravity that holds them present and permanent among the tall firs. The approximately three-hundred-foot-long path through the woods to the guest house resembles a "spirit walk" in a Chinese garden. But instead of memorials to dead ancestors and guardians of the woods, the forest is populated with the playful robustness of the Di Suvero and the brooding weight of the Smith—different but no less potent spirits.

In time, other sculptures will join these or take their place. Knowing that the Wright House was to be more a gallery than a permanent collection,

Erickson and Oberlander avoided making central pedestals that would demand masterpieces. One troublesome location, however, has been the rectangular opening in the terrace between the house and the swimming pool. At first it was planted with a collection of mosses—another echo of the Bloedel Reserve—but the mosses proved too delicate for the realities of daily life, especially the family dogs. Recently, the Wrights commissioned environmental artist Meg Webster to design a piece for the rectangle. The piece, *Conical Depression*, is an inverted cone filled with mosses and other small plants creating a negative space within the positive space of the rectangle.

Despite the strong presence of the surrounding woods, in no way does the landscape design suggest that the Wrights reside in an alien forest or that they are merely barbaric interlopers in nature's domain. The spaces are created by disentangling the essence of a clearing from peripheral distractions. The concreteness of the clearing, its spatial definition, and the Wrights' abstract sculpture are palpable expressions of ideas about natural resources, machines, and the way we can dwell within nature.

PROJECT: **PRIVATE RESIDENCE**

DATE OF COMPLETION: **1979**

LOCATION: **SEATTLE, WASHINGTON**

ARCHITECT: **ARTHUR ERICKSON ARCHITECTS, VANCOUVER OFFICE**
PARTNER-IN-CHARGE: **ARTHUR ERICKSON**
PROJECT TEAM: **NICK MILKOVICH, INARA KUNDZINS, ALLEN CHENG, BOB HOSHIDE, SANDRA FRASER**

LANDSCAPE ARCHITECT: **CORNELIA HAHN OBERLANDER**

STRUCTURAL ENGINEER: **BUSH BOHLMAN & PARTNERS**

MECHANICAL ENGINEER: **D. W. THOMPSON CONSULTANTS**

LIGHTING CONSULTANT: **INCORPORATED CONSULTANTS**

GUEST HOUSE: ARCHITECT: **JAMES CUTLER ARCHITECTS**
LANDSCAPE ARCHITECT: **THOMAS L. BERGER ASSOCIATES, P.S.**

CIGNA

BLOOMFIELD
CONNECTICUT

When it was completed in 1957, the headquarters of Connecticut General Life Insurance Company—now reorganized as CIGNA—was not only one of the first suburban corporate headquarters, but also one of the most widely studied and imitated. Its accuracy and elegance were achieved through a demanding design process that included over 500 client/architect meetings and the construction of a full-scale mock-up of a typical building bay. Many other architects, landscape architects, and corporate officers made pilgrimages to its site in Bloomfield, Connecticut, to study the polished efficiency of its planning and detailing; afterward, most agreed with a reviewer that "the designers refused to be satisfied with what went before as refinement and perfection."[1]

Insurance companies take the long view, and in the early 1950s downtown Hartford offered little room for future expansion. Looking ahead, CIGNA CEO Frazer Wilde and his board of directors foresaw the need for flexible expansion, and architecture and site planning that would accommodate modern office systems. CIGNA wanted the best possible building, in part because they calculated a savings of over $500,000 a year in hiring and turnover costs if employees responded positively to the exodus from the city. Thirty years later, some of Wilde's concerns about uprooting his employees seem quaint. He hoped to assuage their fears of leaving civilization behind by including a pharmacy, a bowling alley, and a barbershop in the suburban headquarters. Assuming that employees who had ridden buses to the downtown office would now depend on a shuttle bus to reach the suburban site, CIGNA initially built only one parking space per two employees. Today, after a

Isamu Noguchi's sculptural group *The Family* resides on a ridge overlooking the lake behind CIGNA's headquarters building.

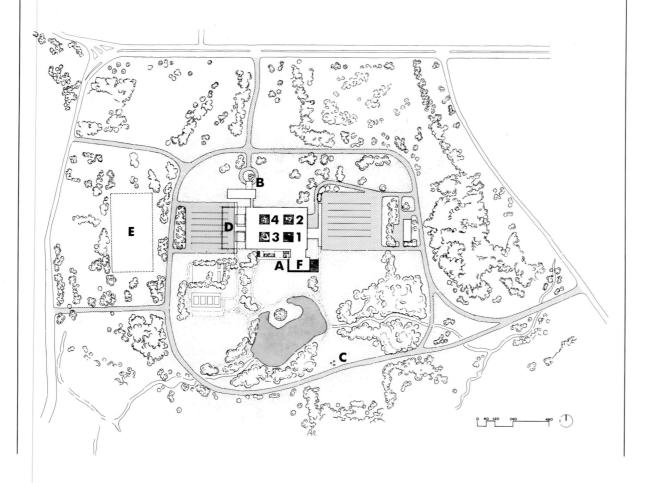

CIGNA

THE BASIC INFORMATION FOR
THIS PLAN WAS PROVIDED BY
THE ARCHITECTS
COLLABORATIVE.

COURTYARDS

1
2
3
4

A. TERRACE
B. BUILDING ENTRANCE
C. ISAMU NOGUCHI,
   THE FAMILY
D. 1972 BUILDING EXPANSION
E. 1972 PARKING GARAGE
F. CAFETERIA WING ABOVE
   REFLECTING POOL

1972 expansion, CIGNA employs over 3,000 people and has increased its parking to 3,000 spaces.

If CIGNA's cautious planning epitomized the corporate client, the architectural firm of Skidmore, Owings & Merrill (SOM) was the epitome of the corporate architecture firm that depends on efficient teamwork to execute large, complex projects throughout the world. Gordon Bunshaft (1909–1990), one of SOM's most creative designers, modestly explained the team approach: "We are a group of ordinary men and women who have the brains to realize that by working together they can achieve more than they could on their own."[2]

CIGNA and SOM considered different strategies before settling on a long, linear building that would allow insurance papers to be passed from one department to the next in assembly-line fashion. The site planning, headed by SOM's landscape architect Joanna Diman, is a model of rational analysis and landscape composition. The building was carefully sited on a low ridge to preserve a number of large oak trees. The edges of the existing masses of other trees were thinned so there would not be an abrupt transition between the lawn areas and the woods. Designed to accommodate future expansion, the landscape was marred only by the large parking lots on either end of the building, which were all the more bleak because CIGNA decided that including any trees would interfere with snow removal.[3] Analyzing the site, engineers found that they could use cool spring water for the HVAC system but would need a lake for excess run-off. Diman widened an existing stream bed and dredged a swampy area in back of the building and carefully constructed a peninsula in order to preserve a huge oak tree.[4]

Bunshaft punctured the 468-foot by 324-foot building with four 72-foot-square interior courtyards to insure that no desk was more than thirty feet from a window. Feeling that the building needed a sculptural counterpoint to the rationality of the architecture, Bunshaft persuaded Wilde to hire artist Isamu Noguchi to help design the courtyards and terrace.

An avid art collector, Bunshaft was contemptuous of both the average architect's interest in art and the average artist's knowledge of architecture, saying that "the only exception would be Noguchi. He knows it all and probably thinks he can be an architect."[5] Bunshaft had first worked with Noguchi on a plaza design for his Lever House, but the plaza was never executed because of budget cuts. At CIGNA Bunshaft persuaded Wilde to pay an advance fee for Noguchi's proposal so that Noguchi would be regarded as an integral member of the design team, not just an artist whose sculpture could be bought or rejected.

Isamu Noguchi (1904–1989) was a protean artist who confounded easy categorization. Besides an extensive oeuvre of sculptures in many different media, Noguchi designed over forty dance sets for Martha Graham and others, dozens of environmental works, lamps, furniture, playgrounds, and fountains. Long before public art became institutionalized by "Percent for Art" and other public art programs in the 1980s, Noguchi fought the prevailing practice that restricted the artist's role to providing a mural or a piece of sculpture to be plopped in front of a building. Public art continues to be less lucrative than gallery sculpture and for years received less recognition. Noguchi once complained that at the dedication of one of his projects, the goldfish were mentioned but not the artist who designed the pool. He was determined to integrate his art into everyday life, denying that "usefulness" and art were ever in conflict. Noguchi considered the sculpture of space as important as that of individual objects. He wrote: "The spaces around buildings should be treated in such a way as to dramatize and make the space meaningful. . . . The sculpting of space may even be invisible as sculpture and still exist as sculptural space."[6]

When collaborating with his artistic equals in other disciplines, Noguchi was often challenged to produce his best work. However, Bunshaft and Noguchi's enormous mutual respect was tempered by stronger individual beliefs in their own work. Bunshaft went to great lengths to guarantee Noguchi's involvement with CIGNA's landscape design, but it was quite clear in his mind who should have the final word: "Collaboration is possible if the client, like Frazer Wilde, is intelligent and open-minded and mutual respect exists. It's the same for the architect and the artist. If both have respect, you might get a damn good building. However, someone has to have the final word. In the case of the building, it is the client. If anyone is working for the architect, the architect has to have to final say."[7] Not surprisingly, Noguchi had a more cynical view, accusing architects of being "egotistical, wanting to hog the whole thing. They are afraid of something that might ruin their building and I think they're justified from experience. . . . I have treated it as a test of my competence to contribute something in spite of so-called collaboration, which is so one-sided."[8]

Bunshaft and Noguchi sustained their collaboration on seven major projects over the course of fifteen years because their artistic triumphs were won not on the playing fields of ego, but through their shared passion for visual clarity, precision, and uncompromising quality in design. CIGNA's courtyards, terrace, and architecture are a wholly consistent world, at once mechanical and organic. Both the architecture and Noguchi's designs are exquisitely detailed and proportioned: in Courtyard One, Noguchi balances the Japanese-derived stepping stones in the water with a straight line of flagstone pavers in the grass; the mechanical perfection of the square pavers is a perfect counterpoint to the flowing organic line of the pool. The pavers point toward—but never reach—the fountain, rendering the water source more distant and mysterious. Noguchi extended the cool classicism of the architecture into an active landscape that escapes from the consistency and repetition of the building module. The building and the landscape are a single piece of art, but the building is *functionally* motivated—it facilitates the insurance company's work—while the courtyards are *aesthetically* motivated, existing primarily to engage the mind and the senses. The courtyards play off the building geometry while the terrace extends it, in part because the terrace accommodates outdoor dining and relaxation.

Bunshaft and Noguchi arrived at this mastery of simplicity and refinement by stripping away the non-essentials. Their collaborative process is partially revealed in the siting of Noguchi's three granite sculptures. Noguchi had proposed that the sculptures be placed on the terrace, and Bunshaft had ordered full-scale plywood mock-ups erected. Bunshaft, Noguchi, and Wilde all agreed that the mock-ups were out of scale. During the ensuing discussion of alternative sites, Wilde proposed placing the sculptures on a rise overlooking the lake. The construction crew promptly hauled them to the ridge, where they perfectly completed Joanna Diman's landscape composition. From the terrace, the flow of space is superbly realized: the cantilevered cafeteria wing and the reflecting pool beneath lead the eye to the lake; and beyond the lake, the woods open to frame Noguchi's sculptures and their reflection in the water. Without the sculpture, the formal diction of the architecture and the terrace

would simply have met the pastoral landscape; instead, the sculpture now orders the flow of space. "Very scientific," Bunshaft quipped. Noguchi later wrote, "I do not deny that the result seems to have justified the dispute, which teaches me never to be tied to preconceptions, to be open to change and chance to the end."[9]

Noguchi was less reconciled to Bunshaft's rejection of one of his courtyard designs. Bunshaft felt that all four courtyards should share a curvilinear design vocabulary, while Noguchi argued that one courtyard should be rectilinear in order to relate to the terrace. Bunshaft finally designed the fourth courtyard himself, but later reflected that "it was probably the worst of the four."[10] Fifteen years later, when the original building was expanded, two more courtyards by SOM were added, so of the six present courtyards, Noguchi designed only three.

CIGNA's courtyards were designed as viewing gardens, since it was assumed that employees would prefer to relax on the terrace or in the cafeteria. As compositions, they are fully revealed from the

Model of Isamu Noguchi's original design for the terrace and four courtyards.
Courtesy of the Isamu Noguchi Foundation, Inc.

CHARLES UHT

The cafeteria wing, which was expanded in 1972, is cantilevered over a reflecting pool.

Isamu Noguchi's design for the terrace encourages social gatherings at lunchtime.

Isamu Noguchi's *The Family* consists of three large granite sculptures, often interpreted as a father, mother, and child.

One of the features of Courtyard Four is this splendid Japanese maple (*Acer palmatum dissectum*).

The Japanese maple shares
the courtyard with a sourwood
(Oxydendron arboreum).

A patriarchal oak tree dominates the pastoral composition designed by landscape architect Joanna Diman.

upper floors, especially Courtyard One with its obvious Japanese references. The flat, planar forms of interlocking water and earth suggest a ying-yang relationship, while the fountain is reminiscent of ritual vessels found in Japanese gardens. In Courtyard Three, buoyancy and gravity, motion and stillness are held in tension. The oval marble bench floats above the ground cover while one long, compound curve of a plane of gravel is played against a shorter arc on the other side.

The courtyards are curvilinear, asymmetrical compositions held in a symmetrical frame. In contrast, Noguchi's terrace extends the rectilinear geometry of the building facade and organizes the space by scale and proportion, offering both seat walls and places for movable chairs and tables.

Often designers consider scale only in the vertical dimension—note the use of scale figures in drawings or photographs—while the horizontal scale is left anemic and stunted. Noguchi understood the importance of horizontal scale in the landscape and deployed broad rectilinear patterns to pull the modular facade onto the terrace.

From the terrace, the lawn sweeps down to the pastoral lake and the patriarchal oak tree. Looming over the far side of the lake, like emissaries from another world, are Noguchi's sculptures. The courtyards and terrace are primarily self-referential compositions that foreground the communication of form and space. In the tradition of English landscape gardens, with their layered references to classical temples, Noguchi's *Family*, as the sculptural group

CIGNA's pastoral landscape, bedecked in fall foliage.

The pristine beauty of the pastoral landscape in winter.

is now known, invites symbolic and metaphysical interpretations. Designed for a business that insures families, the sculpture consists of three figures of rough stony-creek granite, standing sixteen feet, twelve feet, and six feet high respectively. The tall father has a T-shaped crown inscribed with lunar and solar symbols, the mother bears a half moon, and the child presents a combination of the two. Sculpted in the age of atomic bomb scares and family fallout shelters, the figures may be read as symbols of survival.

CIGNA has aged well and has expanded so smoothly that it is impossible to distinguish the original building from its 1972 addition. Its unified design shines with the era's confidence in technology and teamwork—both corporate and artistic—and in the economic and political framework that has allowed this type of architecture and landscape design to endure. Though carefully maintained, the site is not regarded as art by CIGNA and its employees, and the design has suffered as a consequence. Small changes, such as the introduction of a flower bed or the removal of a tree, subvert CIGNA's clarity and precision. Most of the changes could be easily rectified, and one hopes that CIGNA will soon assume a more curatorial role in preserving one of the most influential buildings of the postwar era. While it may not transcend the office environment, with its lyrical accuracy CIGNA's landscape works to clear the mind of the clutter of paperwork and insurance forms, and succeeds in integrating art into daily life.

PROJECT: **CONNECTICUT GENERAL LIFE INSURANCE COMPANY (CIGNA CORPORATION)**

CLIENT: **CONNECTICUT GENERAL LIFE INSURANCE COMPANY (CIGNA CORPORATION)**

DATE OF COMPLETION: **1957**

LOCATION: **BLOOMFIELD, CONNECTICUT**

ARCHITECT: **SKIDMORE, OWINGS & MERRILL**
PARTNER-IN-CHARGE-OF-DESIGN: **GORDON BUNSHAFT**
PARTNER-IN-CHARGE: **WILLIAM S. BROWN**

LANDSCAPE ARCHITECT: **JOANNA C. DIMAN**

ARTIST: **ISAMU NOGUCHI**

GENERAL CONTRACTOR: **TURNER CONSTRUCTION COMPANY**

ELECTRICAL AND MECHANICAL ENGINEER: **SYSKA & HENNESSY**

STRUCTURAL ENGINEER: **WEISKOPF & PICKWORTH**

INTERIOR DESIGN: **KNOLL ASSOCIATES/SOM**

THE DE MENIL HOUSE

**EAST HAMPTON
NEW YORK**

The adherents of modern architecture and landscape architecture believed that they had a vital obligation to solve the problems of modern civilization. Architecture for architecture's sake, or for aesthetic appeal, was distrusted. Students were not told to design beautiful, powerful, or aesthetically pleasing buildings or landscapes; they were given a "problem statement," which described the particular problems the architect or landscape architect were expected to solve.

The architects and landscape architect of the de Menil House on New York's Long Island are firm believers in this rational process. The architects, Charles Gwathmey (1938–) and Robert Siegel (1939–), explain that they approach all projects—from a large hospital to a small house—the same way: "We believe that architecture is generated by the investigation of the specific problem, resulting in a process of ordered calculations . . . all relating to site, orientation, program, circulation, spatial sequence, structure, and technology."[1] With the de Menil House the problem was that there *was* no problem. It was hardly a dilemma, as Gwathmey asserts, "to build a large residence on a private dune site in East Hampton," especially for a wealthy client [like François de Menil] who wants the residence to be "a work of art." This was a tremendous opportunity, Gwathmey acknowledges, "to make a grand summary of the ideas and investigations in the previous houses we had designed on Long Island."[2]

The satellite dish and the ten-foot pink stucco entry wall stand in startling aesthetic contrast to the natural landscape.

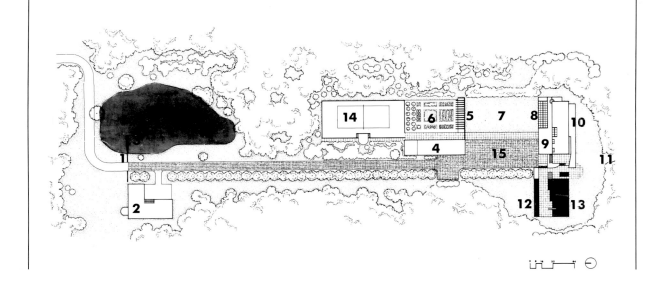

In the absence of any substantial difficulties of function, budget, or site constraints, the designers decided to build a three-story, 11,000-square-foot house that would be an opportunity to respond to Long Island's older shingle-style mansions, which, Gwathmey and Siegel asserted, "were of an appropriate magnitude to anchor their sites and of a scale and presence to allow them to coexist with the ocean and the dunes. [The de Menil House] was an attempt to reinterpret the vernacular shingle-style villa as a modern villa."[3]

Now a problem statement could be formulated. For landscape architect Daniel Stewart (1930–), the problem was "to anchor the very large house in the landscape and to make effective joints between the different zones and between the controlled and natural vegetation."[4] For the architects, the problem was to "recapitulate the ideal intentions of Modernism."[5] A more specific challenge was to use circulation to generate form and the large exterior and interior spaces appropriate to a summer residence or, as Gwathmey put it, "to pull apart the pieces so it will become a place instead of an object."[6]

Modern architects have been embarrassed by such *recherché* indulgences in self-expression or self-referential architectural investigations. In 1965 the journal *Progressive Architecture* chose not to give a single award to any residential design because "It's not a problem at all to design some custom-built

notion of your private palace. . . ."

Ian Laurie, in *An Introduction to Landscape Architecture* (1975), observed that "most contemporary landscape architects have given up designing private gardens" in favor of public projects and large-scale planning. But the Hampton residents themselves had no such puritanical qualms about devouring the latest architectural tour de force. They were, in fact, anticipating the 1980s when architectural stylists became trendy. As an editor of *Progressive Architecture* acknowledged eighteen years after snubbing residential design: "In that cultured playground . . . a new house by a well-known architectural firm is . . . guaranteed to elicit considerable comment from both the local citizenry and from the architectural community."[7]

The architecturally sophisticated Hampton community was created by the newly affluent New Yorkers of the 1960s. They began to summer in the region when new highways made the tip of Long Island an easy drive from Manhattan. Well-educated and cosmopolitan, they were anxious to demonstrate their knowledge of and support for modern art and design. A 1976 *New Yorker* cartoon by William Hamilton showed an architect promising his clients, "In six months you'll have the most powerful architectural statement in the Hamptons."

This part of Long Island is a very private resort with few hotels or public facilities. Most of the modern houses are located in the dunes behind the

The pond's indigenous vegetation forms delicate designs.

incomparable beaches. The isolation of the wind-swept scrub forest and low rolling hills was an ideal setting for the abstraction of modern architecture. Without the architectural context of immediate neighbors, new formal vocabularies could reinterpret the relationship of the summer inhabitants to nature.

The de Menil House is on a twenty-acre site, but only the seven acres farthest from the beach are developed; the acreage between the house and the dunes was donated to the Nature Conservancy, so it may never be developed. Even from the roof deck one is conscious of the beach only as a distant objective hidden behind the secondary and primary dunes. The landscape design is built on this contrast between coarse and smooth and between control and release.

Much of this residence seems excessive, even frivolous. Why build a greenhouse for a summer home or a *brise-soleil* (sun screen) in a mild climate? Only the design team's alertness raises the trifles of summer life—a game of croquet, gin-and-tonics by the pool, a great blue marlin mounted high on the living-room wall—to an expansive and theatrical beauty. Life at the de Menil summer house is amplified by the frame of the *brise-soleil*, which makes the house look even larger, and by the drama of the landscape sequences and events.

Because summer villas are generally intended for entertaining and relaxation, Gwathmey Siegel & Associates and Daniel Stewart decided to use visitor circulation as the engine of their design. The arrival sequence begins as the driveway winds through a drift of black pines and a one-acre pond, surrounded by indigenous vegetation, comes into view. The pond would be unremarkable were it not for the ten-foot-high pink stucco wall projecting into it from the far side. Placed next to the wall, also in the pond, is a television satellite dish, an unusually frank acknowledgment of modern technology. It demonstrates the potential of using the equipment of modern technology in the landscape for aesthetic contrast, a design concept that is far removed from the previous generation of summer residences in the Hamptons.[8]

Had one approached the wall frontally, it would have seemed to be an unusual gateway. Instead, the driveway approach is parallel to the wall, so its opening appears slowly, as if a theatrical curtain were being drawn back. The wall's right side, with its triangular window, engages the caretaker's house behind. These improvisational gestures reassure us that the designers have something more conscious in mind than simply pilfering the signature mystical walls of the great Mexican architect Luis Barragán.

Once we have driven through this first curtain of the arrival sequence, we head up a long driveway flanked on one side by thirty-eight linden trees. The tactility of the cobblestone driveway, grass poking between the stones, slows the eye. Further up the drive, which crests slightly at this point, the guest house comes into view on the left, just before the landscape dramatically opens up to reveal an enormous gray wall enclosing a large greenhouse with a peaked roof. The cobblestone drive widens and terminates in an auto court. To the left of the auto court is the billiard-table-smooth surface of the croquet court. Another pink stucco wall, this time a full frontal expression, leads off to the right.

If we were to park the car and walk beneath a projecting second-story balcony, we would first discover a swimming pool on the other side of the pink wall. Ahead, continuing along the same axis, the lawn abruptly descends into a rectangular opening in the dense dune vegetation. It is as if there were a secret door, for only the most rudimentary path leads through the secondary and primary dunes to the beach. The indigenous vegetation is scruffy and windblown, with juniper, scrub pines, and rosa rugosa huddled together in a five-to-eight-foot-high, thick forest. This is sometimes called a "sunken forest" because the height of the surrounding dunes and the density of the wind-buffeted hollies, pitch pines, and sassafras make one feel submerged beneath the rolling dunes. Only when one rises to the top of a dune can one turn to see the great outline of the house, riding like an ocean liner on what F. Scott Fitzgerald, in *The Great Gatsby,* called "the fresh, green breast of the new world."

Our arrival at the beach marks the final landscape zone. Serendipitously, glacial deposits of garnet have left streaks of pink and red in the sand. We have moved through different natures: a wild pond punctuated with exotic walls and technology, an allée of linden trees, the *tapis vert* of the croquet court, the tropical forest in the greenhouse, the plane of the swimming pool and slate pool deck, the dense dunes, and finally the light and vast expanse of the ocean.

The site plan of the de Menil House, like Kiley's Miller House (see pages 112–27), is a nine-square organization with the arrival axis parallel to the entrance of the house. Marked by a green slate walk between the croquet court and the auto court, the front door is an erosion in the house's weathered-gray facade. The slate walk also defines a second axis leading to the cutting garden, the guest house, and the tennis court.

From the front door, interior circulation is layered from north to south: the greenhouse is the first layer and the *brise-soleil* the last. The greenhouse is not the inhabitable space the facade might lead us to expect; instead, it is a green wall of ficus, philodendron, and other plants, as if the horizontal green plane of the croquet court had been pulled perpendicular and brought inside.

The house's interior circulation leads up the stairs to the roof deck, which is framed by the *brise-soleil* and given dimension by the chimneys protruding through the roof. Here one feels in control of the vast dune landscape and the horizon lines of the ocean, which sail off as far as the eye can see. The white, nautically inspired handrails complete the architect's faithful and affectionate bow to Le Corbusier, who urged designers to emulate the sleek, functional designs of ocean liners and airplanes. Looking down from the roof deck, one also surveys the pink wall enclosing the deep

The satellite dish makes a bold statement about the use of modern technological equipment in the landscape.

The cobblestone driveway leading to the house is flanked on the right by a row of linden trees. The area on the left was originally intended to replicate the indigenous landscape.

View from the entrance of the house toward the grape arbor and cutting garden. The croquet lawn is on the right, the auto court on the left. In the distance is the guest house.

blue swimming pool, with its attendant population of white lounge chairs. From the grand sweep of the roof deck, the Long Island beach and the tropical paradise symbolized by the pink walls seem equally near and distant—like hazy memories of two grand summer holidays.

We can descend to the swimming pool by the exterior stairway. The scale of these stairs and the dimensions of the swimming pool balance the commanding roof deck perfectly. These and other feats of equilibrium are the payoff resulting from all the other Hampton homes that Gwathmey and Siegel designed. Out of that work came a naturalness, an accustomed mastery of proportion and scale as well as, in the de Menil House, elaborations and reversals of previous strategies.

Feats of equilibrium are also apparent in the landscape design, which rejects the symmetry of grand old estates, but not their large spaces. Daniel Stewart explains that "we wanted to anchor the house to the site by scale, not by fiddling around with the foundation of the building or the pink walls."[9] The croquet court pulls the fifty-three-foot facade of the house onto the site and at the same time pivots the orientation of the landscape toward the looser planting on the other side of the drive.

There are some telling details, such as the blue rails that spring off the arbor structure next to the croquet court, recalling the nautical imagery of the house. And the alley created by the rose fence and the east side of the guest house, through which one has to squeeze, is a domesticated version of the path through the "sunken forest" to the beach. But on the whole, the virtues of the landscape are in its broad organization. The ancillary spaces—particularly the tennis court and the cutting garden—are diagrammatic and flat, lacking the transparencies and layerings that make the circulation through the house such a rich spatial experience.

With its finely calibrated zoning, jointing, transparencies, and framing, the de Menil House is like a great clock. It has a clock's beauty and impersonal mechanical perfection: a cool and elegant accouterment to a summer's pleasure away from the grit of Manhattan. In less than ten years the villa has been sold twice and the wild vegetation around the entrance pond has been tamed, weakening the contrasting forms of the pink wall, the satellite dish, and the wildflowers.

The de Menil House is an exercise in the art of architecture at its least mystical. The problems of arrival, procession, scale, joining, and layering are all the problems design students must master, but seldom with such sophisticated grace. The experience was so instructional to François de Menil that he decided to study architecture. In time, the de Menil House will become part of the history of the Hamptons and a challenge to twenty-first-century designers, just as its designers were challenged by the shingle-style villas of their forebears.

In this view of the house and swimming pool the masterful balance of the design is clearly evident.

A large oculus penetrates the *brise-soleil* that frames the roof garden, which looks out over the six acres of dunes separating the house from the beach.

The swimming pool wall and the lily pond in front of it form a sophisticated, abstract composition. OPPOSITE

The cutting garden next to the guest house.

PROJECT: **PRIVATE RESIDENCE**

DATE OF COMPLETION: **1979**

LOCATION: **EAST HAMPTON, NEW YORK**

ARCHITECT: **GWATHMEY SIEGEL & ASSOCIATES**

ASSOCIATE ARCHITECT: **BRUCE D. NAGEL**

LANDSCAPE ARCHITECT: **DANIEL D. STEWART & ASSOCIATES**

GENERAL CONTRACTOR: **JOHN TURNER**

MECHANICAL ENGINEER: **JEFFERIES ENGINEERING**

MASTER PLAN FOR DESERT HIGHLANDS: **GAGE DAVIS ASSOCIATES**

LIGHTING: **CHA DESIGN**

LANDSCAPE CONTRACTORS: **LEWIS & VALENTINE**

THE MILLER HOUSE

A TOWN IN THE MIDWEST

The Miller House is suffused with a love and understanding of history, but also with a determination to live fully in the modern world. As architectural historian David Streatfield noted: "There is a deliciously exciting poetic sense of the spirit of the past living again in the present and refreshing it, sort of surging through it."[1] At the same time, the Miller House is one of America's first truly contemporary residential landscape designs to reject the revival solutions or the eclecticism that had dominated American estates in the first half of the twentieth century.

The Miller House is situated in the margins of an ordinary suburb on the outskirts of a small midwestern town, but it is indicative of the true nature of the house that the first publication about it was titled "A Contemporary Palladian Villa."[2] Traditionally, a villa is defined as a house in the country—a *villa urbana,* if it is not part of an agricultural estate—designed for the owner's enjoyment and relaxation, but the term further implies the owner's economic privilege and aspiration to patronize the arts. Though the Miller House is firmly rooted in the history of Palladian villas and formal European gardens, the client's enlightened patronage of modern architecture—manifested in his sponsorship of nationally known architects for the design of public buildings in his hometown—enabled its designers to imbue the house and the landscape with modernism's great gift of space and grace. The house is such a rich depository of ideas and small design decisions—all freighted with signifi-

At the north end of the honey locust allée, Henry Moore's *Draped Reclining Woman* (1957–58) appears to be surveying the broad lawn to the right.

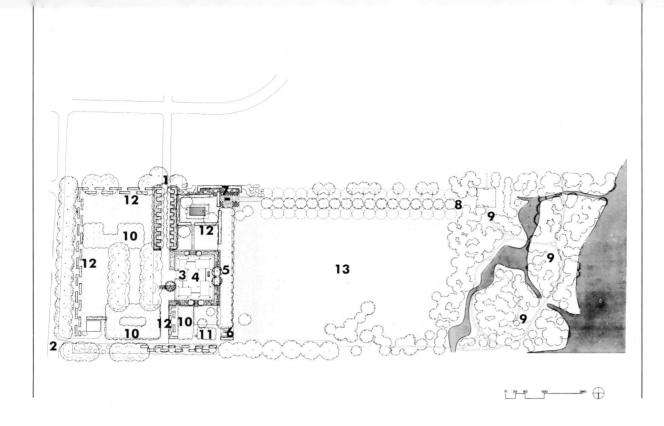

cance—that, like all great art, it is accessible on many different levels and repays the effort of repeated visits and examination.

For most of history, concepts of villa design have been predicated upon a close relationship between the country and the city. Villas are also designed for the particular needs and aesthetic sensibilities of their clients. As architecture historian James Ackerman observes: "What gave Palladio freedom and inspiration to build exciting structures was the knowledge of the boundaries in which he had to maneuver—the tradition of the distant or immediate past, the specific demands of clients, the choice of materials and of a site."[3] The Miller House gave landscape architect Dan Kiley (1912–   ) the opportunity to achieve the most perfect realization of his philosophy that "man *is* nature." The ideology of the client, who is a successful businessman in a very small, conservative midwestern town, deeply informed the making of the villa, particularly in the sumptuous virility of its materials, the careful attention to details, and the way it addresses its neighbors. His ideology also accounts for some of the shortcomings of the house—both in its maintenance and in its incompletion.

The architect of the Miller House, Eero Saarinen (1910–1961), and landscape architect Dan Kiley first worked together on the St. Louis Arch competition in 1946. By the time work began on the Miller House in 1952, their respective firms were fully established and primarily engaged with large institutional or corporate clients—Kiley and Saarinen were collaborating on Dulles Airport and New Jersey's Bell Laboratories while the Miller House was under construction. Encumbered by the programmatic and technical exigencies of these large projects, Saarinen, Kiley, interior architect Alexander Girard, and Saarinen's young associate Kevin Roche took great pleasure and pride in their extraordinary opportunity to craft the villa carefully over a five-year period. Roche, who worked on many more projects for Mr. Miller, most appreciated Miller's willingness to "bend over backwards to try and *understand* what you were trying to do. Too many clients just tell you if they like it, but you never know if they understand it."[4]

The architecture is so completely modern—featuring a grid of freestanding white cruciform steel columns, long skylights bringing natural, diffused light to the interior, a round fireplace, and a quintessential but exceptionally elegant 1950s

Large taxus hedges frame the service entrance to the property.

Detail of the wire-mesh glass panels that mask the parking area from the service area on the east side of the house.

lounge or conversation pit—that it is easy to overlook the structure's important historical precedents. Like Palladio's Villa Foscari, built circa 1559–60 and known as the Malcontenta, the rooms and services are organized around a central space within a nine-square grid. The critical difference is that the Malcontenta was symmetrically composed with the central space dominant, while the perimeter rooms of Saarinen's villa are offset, displacing the hierarchy of rooms with a more egalitarian and functional arrangement.

The contrasting architectural organizations, or *parti*, of the Villa Foscari and the Miller House are informed by the different ideologies of their respective centuries and cultures. The symmetrical plan of the Malcontenta was determined by Palladio's belief in the mathematical perfection of musical harmony. Sixteenth-century Italians held that nature was revealed in harmonic progressions, so the perfect proportions of the Malcontenta mirrored the natural order of nature. In addition, its heavy walls, great portico, and imposing central room affirmed the owner's powerful position in society and the more general position of man as center of the universe. In the Miller House, the spaces of the building and the landscape do flow from a single source, as if man were their sole reason for existence, but the geometry of the landscape is additive, with the space always evolving just when a classical garden would have narrowed the focus to a single terminus. The designers of the Miller House did not use geometry to model the world in a central room or a single vista; their careful displacement of geometry reveals their concern for the play of shadow, light, and space.

The owners of the 7,600-square-foot Miller House did not want to give the impression of walling off the property from their neighbors; nevertheless they wanted to protect their privacy. Kiley's solution was to enclose the front yard with staggered segments of ten-foot-high arborvitae hedges, interspersed originally with red maples, which were later removed when they began to shade out the hedges. Although this boundary design is physically penetrable, passersby can't see into the yard. In back, however, there are no barriers of any kind between the Millers' property and their neighbors'.

The clients' modesty also dictated that the house not be an imposing object in the landscape, and indeed, the villa is not visible when one enters the estate through a dense tunnel of horse chestnuts. Bordered by broad, horizontal bands of low taxus shrubs and vinca minor, the driveway runs parallel to the house, toward a weeping beech tree and a translucent screen that separates the service side from the guest parking. Appropriate to a modern villa, the carport is carved from the block of the house, and a generous fifty-foot-wide area for guest parking extends from inside the carport. The central interior space opens to the landscape on only one side, while the long band of skylights next to the wall bathes the room in natural light. To the north and south are the blocks of rooms that anchor each corner of the house.

Saarinen and Kiley used the same spatial order so that the architecture and the landscape are completely integrated in an atmospheric circulation, yet the house does not extend into the landscape nor does the landscape present a dramatic picture from inside the house—the house and the landscape are one and the same. The sixteen cruciform steel columns that support the villa all stand apart from the walls, so the flat roof appears to float above the rooms and the columns on the perimeter merge with the tree trunks, integrating the structure and movement of the house with that of the landscape.

No trees existed on the original ten-acre site, which was divided by a sharp change in elevation from a higher plateau near the street to a 2,100-foot-long meadow and floodplain below. The views to the west—at the rear of the villa—are expansive, overlooking a small river that frequently floods its shallow banks. Kiley surrounded the house with interlocking grids of trees, lawns, and ground covers, all of which, in his words, extend the architecture "outward in layers to the limits of the site on three sides and to the west to confront the natural meadow. The sense of spaces unfolding and opening to join with one another inside is repeated outside, linking the house to the landscape."[5]

A marble plinth extends ten feet from the walls

of the house on three sides, and ivy ground cover extends the plinth fifteen feet. Paths penetrate through the horizontal planes of ground cover into the lawn and other areas. On the north side of the house, the cool dining-room side, the plinth is not merely a terrace abutting a lawn but an outdoor room with a passage to other outdoor rooms: a square lawn area, a bosque of crab apples, and a bosque of redbuds. The south side, which includes the TV room and children's quarters, has an inviting green lawn with a bluestone path leading directly to the swimming pool. And on the west side of the house, two magnificent weeping beech trees rest on the villa like gentle vegetative giants. Kiley's design extends the plinth and surrounds the building with outdoor enclosures, so that the building is alive

along its entire circumference, drawing us willingly around its periphery.

Perhaps Kiley's most inspired geometry at the Miller House is the allée of honey locusts running parallel to the house on the western side. Contrary to expectation, the allée does not lead from the house to the floodplain but serves as an esplanade—the locust trunks are the posts and the tree canopy is the roof—overlooking the meadow. Kiley used drains between every other locust tree to enable the ground plane to be absolutely level instead of being sloped toward a few drains.[6] So the allée is as horizontal as the marble plinth on which the house stands, making it an extension of the same aesthetic as the house. Standing within this esplanade, one simultaneously occupies a strongly direc-

Instead of three rows of sycamores, as Dan Kiley originally planned, a single row of red maples leads toward the steps and the small pool at the south end of the honey locust allée. OPPOSITE

View of the Henry Moore sculpture from the west side of the house. During the winter cut boughs protect the ivy ground cover that surrounds the house on three sides.

Like the rest of the landscape and the house, this crab apple bosque is organized in a grid. The tulips are the Millers' personal touch. OVERLEAF

tional allée and has a framed view of the long meadow and wetlands below.

Kiley and Miller could not agree on a design for the north end of the allée. Miller rejected all of Kiley's proposals and decided to "live with it" before making a decision. Ten years later, Kevin Roche designed a small orangery, but Miller decided that a building would disrupt the spatial flow of the garden.[7] A few years later, the Millers purchased

Henry Moore's *Draped Reclining Woman* (1957–58), which they positioned on a shallow podium.

The south end terminates in a small square pool and discreet water jet, behind which the Millers recently installed a bas relief by Jacques Lipchitz. The south end of the allée also acts as a hinge connecting the honey locusts to what was planned to be a triple allée of sycamores and is now a single row of red maples. One descends from the

square pool down a wide staircase with shallow three-inch risers to the row of red maples leading to the floodplain. For that area, Kiley designed a lush, romantic park with some contemporary sculpture, in contrast to the rest of the landscape, because "it wouldn't have been appropriate to do geometry there [with] the seasonal flooding" and because the area is "so far from the house."[8] The conjunction of a wild garden with the formal garden of the house is often found in Italian villas, and the park's inclusion would have philosophically completed Kiley's vision—"man is nature." But it was never executed, primarily because the inevitable dishevelment of the statues and paths in the flood-prone area was foreign to the Millers' aesthetic sensibilities. Today the wetlands are a visual rather than experiential counterpoint to the geometry surrounding the villa.

The owners have lavished immaculate care on the villa, but have made some questionable decisions. A second bosque of crab apples has replaced the bosque of redbuds next to the Henry Moore statue. Lost is the wonderful contrast of the airy redbuds with the denser crab apples and with it, some of the delightful modulation and surprise that humanize Kiley's geometry. The envisioned color and sweep of the wildflower meadow or the lower level was exchanged for a large suburban lawn, perhaps in deference to the neighbors. Less reversible is the planting of a single row of red maples, spaced twenty-seven feet apart, along the meadow, in lieu of Kiley's original call for three rows of sycamores twenty feet apart, because the Millers liked viewing an expansive lawn. The present lawn is very broad indeed by most suburban standards and would have been a more positive space had it

Weeping willow trees grace the broad, expansive lawn.

Geometry orders the
landscape and frames the
natural forms of the trees.

The honey locust allée runs parallel to both the vast lawn (left) and the house. One of the enormous weeping beech trees that tower over the house can be seen at the right.

been bordered by the triple allée. This simple matter of one row of trees versus three rows is what often distinguishes Kiley's designs: Where more timid or less persuasive landscape architects would have planted one row, he would plant three, which might be enough to turn a banal experience into an extraordinary one.

Like the house, the landscape is organized in a nine-square composition, which differs significantly from the four-square composition of classical gardens. The basic difference between a four-square composition and a nine-square composition is that the former creates a point at the center where the four squares meet; in classical gardens, this point

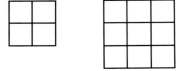

becomes a statue, fountain, or other object. A composition of nine squares has an open square at the center, making the open space—not an object—the dominant compositional element.

The importance of this organization in the Miller House is most apparent in the placement of the driveway between the open lawn and the house

Behind the small fountain at the south end of the honey locust allée is Jacques Lipchitz's bas relief *Man with Guitar* (1923).

In summer the honey locusts' leaves form a canopy over the allée.

so that the latter is occupying a "square" instead of being the termination of a path. The locust allée, by its parallel relationship to the house, is also one of the spaces in the nine-square composition, even though it is linear. On a smaller scale, the bosque of apple trees is planted in a nine-square composition with the trees removed from the center square. A four-square composition with a statue or other object in the center could never be as apt for a modern landscape as that simple square of sunshine cast on the green lawn.

While few can fail to be moved by the vibrancy of Kiley's geometry, many equate modern formalism with a domination of nature. Kiley responds passionately to such claims by insisting that his approach recognizes and celebrates nature. "Real nature is wonderful because it is such a tremendous experience. Instead of three or four different types of trees in stupid little clumps, you might have five million aspens or sugar maples. Landscape architects are always making little imitations of nature instead of the real thing."[9] As the eighteenth-century visionary French architect Etienne-Louis Boullée proclaimed: "The task of architecture is to implement nature, not imitate her."

Kiley is, above all, a radical empiricist, and insists that his designs can be validated only by someone who has walked through them. Kiley's designs are a search for structure and movement. He says, "Movement is ever-continuous and elusive, like a maze. Dynamic movement that ends, but extends to infinity. It's a mystic quality of space developed by the order of trees and other landscape things . . . every time you walk in nature it is a fresh experience. You might squeeze through some small maple trees, pick your way across a rushing stream and climb up a hill into an open meadow. It's always moving and changing spatially. . . . What I've been trying to do is create a man-made scene having those spatial qualities."[10]

There is a common perception that such highly organized gardens lack passion or life. But, as pianist Rosalyn Tureck once replied to charges that Bach's music was so formal and cerebral that it lacked the passion of the romantic composers: "When you have something well structured, all your emotions can pour through this structure. It frees you to respond emotionally. The more clarity there is the more open the fountain of feeling becomes."[11]

PROJECT: **THE MILLER HOUSE**

DATE OF COMPLETION: **1955**

LOCATION: **THE MIDWESTERN UNITED STATES**

ARCHITECTS: **EERO SAARINEN AND ASSOCIATES WITH ALEXANDER GIRARD**
PRINCIPAL-IN-CHARGE: **EERO SAARINEN**
PROJECT MANAGER: **KEVIN ROCHE**

LANDSCAPE ARCHITECT: **DAN KILEY**

INTERIOR DESIGN: **ALEXANDER GIRARD**

THREE

MODERN NARRATIVES

The word *narrative* derives from the Latin *gnarus*, which can be translated "knowing," "familiar with." Narrative is not a plot with a beginning and an end or a temporal sequence of events, but the way in which one understands the world. The plot may tell one what happened next, but the narrative is how we understand why it happened. Most agree on the plot of the Old Testament, for example, but there is wide disagreement on its narrative. There are a great many different narrative modes, but with regard to the designs in this section, the most relevant ones are the classical narrative and the modern narrative.

A designer working in the classical narrative mode tries to clearly communicate a particular idea, usually by relying on symbols. A good example is the Bethesda Fountain in New York's nineteenth-century Central Park. Bethesda was the name of a basin in ancient Jerusalem that healed the sick, and Olmsted, the designer of the park, used this biblical symbol to convey his message that the park was performing a healing or cleansing role in the city.[1] Today, few people understand the symbolism of the fountain, and although it is certainly specious to argue that it is not possible to love and enjoy a landscape unless one understands it, the classical narrative has become increasingly less effective in our pluralistic society.

Many modern designers concluded that classical references to obsolete cultures or traditions were no longer universally known and were irrelevant to a scientific age. Some psychologists and anthropologists maintained, however, that there were archetypal symbols such as sun and shade or circles and squares whose understanding did not depend on historical knowledge. This led to a

modern conception of narrative that uses both archetypal symbols and knowledge of the physical qualities of a particular region and its culture. People's capacity to comprehend the narrative is honed by living in that particular climate and culture. The designer can construct a landscape with these regional characteristics so that the physical experience of the design leads to an understanding of the narrative. Thus the Fuller House in Arizona holds deep meaning for those who live in the desert and Ira's Fountain is deeply appreciated by the people of Portland, who have experienced the Columbia River dams and the cataracts of the nearby Cascades. What these designs have in common is that the designers have taken the ordinary experience of the people and used it to create a landscape design that is valued more for what it is and how it is experienced than for what it might refer to or symbolize. Visitors lacking local knowledge can still grasp the universal elements of the narrative, such as the pyramids and circles in the Fuller House. But none of the designs in this section depends on *a posteriori* knowledge of literary texts, religious symbols, or historical events.

A particular challenge for designers of narrative landscapes is the question of time—both the actual passage of time and the time it takes to experience the narrative. The Crosby Arboretum, for instance, structures our experience with stage directions—both written, in the arboretum's interpretive literature, and physical, in the slow twists and turns of the path system. Like all modern narratives, the Crosby Arboretum is an attempt to communicate deep human meaning without abstruse symbols or prior knowledge.

THE FULLER HOUSE

S C O T T S D A L E
A R I Z O N A

The Pueblo people of the American Southwest have maintained their traditions through many centuries, even in the face of modernization. Their landscape is open and their buildings are massed together in a sensible climatic adaptation, but their settlement patterns and architecture are more than simple ecological responses. Architecture historian Vincent Scully has observed that the environmental design of Pueblo villages recapitulates their creation myths and the massing of the buildings creates spaces for sacred dances and rituals. Scully cautions against applying Western ideas about distinctions between nature and culture to the Pueblos: "There exists no discrimination between nature and man as such, but only an ineradicable instinct that all living things are one. And all are living: snake, mountain, cloud, eagles, and men."[1]

Today the organic integrity of the remaining Pueblo villages may be seen as a telling indictment of the chaos and sprawl of modern southwestern cities. Recoiling from the detritus of their consumerist culture, some city residents have looked to the compelling starkness of the desert for an antiquity and authenticity their own culture so painfully lacks.

The Fuller House in Scottsdale, Arizona, is located on the plateau at the base of the MacDowell Mountain Range, not far from Frank Lloyd Wright's Taliesin West. The landscape is dry and roughly strewn with boulders, and the spiky limbs and small sharp leaves of the shrubs and trees are aggressive yet delicate, simultaneously fragile and unyielding. Blue palo verde, mesquite, ironwood, and ocotillo

The circular pool and the pyramid are not only strong design elements but powerful, archetypal symbols as well.

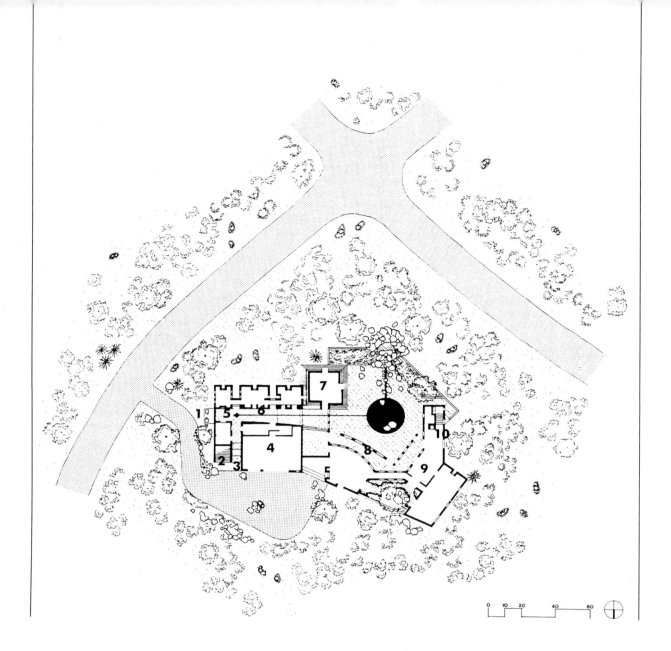

screen the house from the road, while a half-dozen saguaro cacti stand sentinel in front. But unlike the vast acreage of Taliesin West, the 5,500-square-foot Fuller House occupies only three-quarters of an acre on a corner lot. It is one of many houses in Desert Highlands, a densely settled 860-acre residential and recreational community.

The fact that the Fuller House looks and feels as if it were situated in a vast desert is a tribute to the Master Plan of Desert Highlands' landscape architects Gage Davis Associates. Determined to insinuate the development harmoniously into the pristine desert environment, Davis helped draft rigorous deed restrictions. By limiting construction

disturbances and mandating revegetation, these development restrictions preserve the visual and tactile continuum of the indigenous landscape. There are no sidewalks, no curbs or gutters, and no street lights; even the tennis courts are unlit to preserve night views. Where disturbances were unavoidable, an extraordinary preconstruction transplant program salvaged over 1,200 saguaro cacti, 600 large palo verdes, and thousands of brittlebush, bursage, and jojoba. Phil Hebets directed the revegetation at the Fuller House, which included carefully sowing annual grasses to restore the desert's ability to resist invasive plants. Without Gage Davis's commitment to the preservation of the desert environ-

The sunset tower and pyramid as seen from the road. This landscape differs considerably from the conventional front lawns found in older residential areas of Scottsdale.

Octillos, blue palo verdes, brittlebush, and tall saguaro cacti flourish in the Desert Highlands landscape. To those who think of deserts as barren, the lushness of the vegetation comes as a surprise.

The open channel in the long gallery inside the house carries water toward the courtyard. The window grilles cast lattice-patterned shadows on the rough-cut adoquín stone floor.

ment, it might have been impossible for architect Antoine Predock (1936–   ) to forge a physical and spiritual connection between the Fuller House and the larger landscape.

The Fuller House was to be a contemporary home for its owners, who are leaders in the Phoenix business community. Predock's concept for the house was to "merge an image of this powerful, surreal landscape with an evocation of the area's cultural stratigraphy to produce an architecture that transcends both historicism and regionalism.'[2] This mediation between the conveniences and comforts of a universal modern culture and elements indirectly derived from the local culture and landscape has been called "critical regionalism" by architecture historian Kenneth Frampton, though "empathetic regionalism" might better describe Predock's strategy.[3] The architect grounded the Fuller House in the Pueblo people's concordance with nature, in the daily path of the sun, in the realities of the site's ecology, and in the Spanish concept of *sol y sombra*—sun and shade—the extreme conditions of a desert environment.[4]

Driving through Desert Highlands, one catches a glimpse of a mysterious rosy pyramid with a dark glass apex amid the house's ensemble of flat-roofed greenish-beige stucco blocks. One loses sight of the pyramid as the Fuller driveway swings past two piers of the same rosy complexion. In between the piers, water jets inscribe a lattice pattern—a motif that is repeated throughout the property. And, through a narrow slit in the wall of the house, one can glimpse a black stone fountain and a channel of water. The entrance to the house is recessed between the garage and a set of stairs leading up to an outdoor pavilion.

One enters and descends into a long gallery, where one encounters the block of black polished granite with a sheen of water welling on its top. The water drapes itself over the sides of the granite and is guided into a long channel leading to the end of the gallery. The floor is of the same material as the pyramid and the twin piers—a rough-cut Mexican adoquín stone. The entire gallery is recessed into the desert, and in the dining, breakfast, and kitchen rooms to the left, windows are at eye level with the gila monsters, lizards, and other inhabitants of the desert floor. The house is like a burrow, albeit a very large one. The water leads down two short sets of steps to a window wall covered with thick aluminum grilles for protection from the sun at the end of the hall, and on the left is an arched entry to the pyramid, which turns out to be the Fullers' study.

At this end of the gallery it becomes apparent that the house is a three-sided enclosure for a courtyard and circular pool; the gallery water channel runs beneath the window wall to the pool. Facing the gallery on the other side of the courtyard is the master bedroom and, above it, an open tower. Connecting the bedroom wing to the rest of the house is a curved loggia. A second water channel emerges from the courtyard wall—as if from the desert itself—and intersects with the first at the pool. These two water channels are the main axes of the house and landscape.

The masses of salvia, myoporum, and other ground covers along the low wall effectively allow the courtyard to flow into the desert, and the boulders that tumble into the courtyard and the pool also bridge the two realms. In contrast to the black stone in the interior gallery, the water source in the courtyard is all but invisible among the pile of rocks and the vegetation. Its axis points to a tall saguaro (recently a gila woodpecker made a nest in the saguaro and this yawning cavity creates a felicitous visual connection to the circular pool). The avalanche of boulders is less successful; it comes very close to the preciousness of a miniature golf course and lacks the authenticity and substance of the larger landscape and architectural elements.

The archetypal power of the Fuller House is revealed only with the full experience of the diurnal cycle. The morning sun rises over the sunrise pavilion and streams into the breakfast room and bedroom. During the day, the glass-topped pyramid tracks time around the stepped edges of its ceiling. At sunset, the changing desert colors are best savored from the sunset tower above the master bedroom, and after sunset, the pyramid offers night views of the Phoenix skyline. Late at night, from the heroically scaled bed in the master bedroom, one can

The sleek black granite fountain in the gallery is as soothing to the eye as its coolness is to the touch.

watch the moon rise above the pyramid until its reflection is captured in the circular pool. Predock describes this distillation of the diurnal cycle as "architecture and landscape, daily life and natural cycles, joining in synchronous dances."[5]

The joy experienced in discovering these multiple views of the desert exemplifies what geographer Jay Appleton calls the "prospect-refuge theory."[6] Appleton theorizes that since the ability to see without being seen is favorable to biological survival, it is a source of deep, innate pleasure. A prospect is a long view, so a desert is a "prospect-dominant" landscape, while a dense forest is refuge-dominant. In the forest one seeks a longer view, while in the desert, the first instinct is for refuge. At the Fuller House, the daytime sun is fierce, so it is with great relief that one ducks into the canyon or burrow of the gallery. Later, in the cool of the evening, one emerges cautiously from the house's refuge to gain a panoramic prospect from the sunset tower, which surveys both the house itself and the Desert Highlands community beyond.

Predock alluded to Pueblo architecture in the stepped ledges of the pyramid, which also echoes some of the jagged peaks of the surrounding mountains. It is no coincidence that the language of the Hopi, one of the Pueblo tribes, uses te'wi for both "steps," as in a building, and "ledge," as on a mountain; like the pyramid of the Fuller House, the mass of the densely packed Pueblo settlements has a natural consonance with the shapes of the surrounding mountains.

Of course, the pyramid is also an archetypal form—the world mountain—and is found in many cultures throughout the world. Like Egyptian pyramids, the base of the Fuller pyramid is squared to the compass points. Its glass apex is similar to the polished black or quartz stones that often topped Egyptian pyramids to catch the first and last rays of the sun. The glass apex might also call to mind the open eye at the apex of the pyramid on the back of the American dollar bill, a Masonic symbol suggesting the unfinished work of the nation.

The pyramid is juxtaposed to an equally fecund symbol—the circular pool. In Western culture, the circle is traditionally a symbol of heaven and unity, while the pyramid and the square—the base of the pyramid—are earthbound forms, the realm of cities and other built environments. Their conjunction in the courtyard forms the perceptual and spiritual center of the house.

The potential pretentiousness of such heavily symbolic forms is mitigated by Predock's whimsical elaborations of the pyramidal motif. The Fullers have delighted in discovering pyramids or triangles throughout the house. The glass apex casts triangular shadows, as do the triangular grilles that cover the windows and that form the roofs of the pavilion and tower. The motif is especially felicitous in the sunset tower, where the roof grille casts a

The second water channel emerges from the boulders near the courtyard wall. The disposition of these boulders dissolves the boundary between the hard pavement of the courtyard and the desert landscape on the other side of the wall.

Brittlebush (*Encelia farinosa*).

Desert marigolds (*Baileya multiradiata*).

The Fuller House pyramid echoes the shape of the mountain beyond.

bifurcated silhouette against its smooth stucco walls. These insubstantial shadow pyramids shimmer in the desert heat and contrast with the solid fact of the stone pyramid across the courtyard.

But all these small pleasures and delights do not negate the sacredness inherent in the mythically laden pyramids and circles. After all, the Fuller House was designed for clients who wanted more than the domestic habitat of a characterless suburban house. They have chosen to live in a house poised between quotidian activities and the profundity of the desert, between modern and ancient cultures.

The physical contact with water and stone informs the central narrative of the Fuller House— that of earth and water. The different ways in which we encounter water at the Fuller House lead to an

understanding of its centrality and spiritual importance in desert cultures. Water is first encountered in the twin piers of adoquín stone, which suggest the breaking open of the earth to release the water's flow. Once inside the entrance hall, few can resist touching the cool water on the sleek black granite stone, performing an unconscious ablution. Both water and adoquín stone continue through the gallery and into the courtyard, where the rosy pyramid evokes both the MacDowell Mountains and the desert floor. At its apex, the blue glass skylight offers another hint of water. Near a small fire pit in the boulders crowding the courtyard wall, the other water channel emerges. Fire, water, the mountains, and the sky all converge at the circular pool, which literally reflects what Predock calls the "poetic tension in the gentle standoff between built

The purple and red flowers of autumn sage (*Salvia greggii*) complement the rose-colored stone of the pyramid.

The desert landscape at sunset.

forms and the desert environment."

For Predock, the power of the Fuller House "emanates from the amalgamation of landform, climate, [and] light, . . . from a composite of physical artifacts and palpable spiritual forces. The elements of the landscape—the geology, violent diurnal and seasonal temperature extremes, and the highly variable quality of light—interact continually."[7] The Fuller House transcends historicism by fully embracing the desert's own particular light. In the morning, blues and grays are called up by the shadows of the rising sun. At midday, the landscape becomes almost monochromatic in the intensity of the desert sun. In the late afternoon, color gradually returns—first to the rosy pavement of the courtyard, and then to the greenish-beige stucco walls. Finally, in the cool of the evening, darkness gradually closes over the many layers of culture and nature—water and stone, prospect and refuge, *sol y sombra*, the timeless grandeur of the desert and the distant lights of Phoenix—that comprise the narrative of the Fuller House.

P R O J E C T : **PRIVATE RESIDENCE**

L O C A T I O N : **DESERT HIGHLANDS, SCOTTSDALE, ARIZONA**

D A T E   O F   C O M P L E T I O N : **1986**

A R C H I T E C T : **ANTOINE PREDOCK ARCHITECT**

P L A N T I N G : **SONORA DESERT LANDSCAPING**
PRESIDENT: **PHIL HEBETS**

G E N E R A L   C O N T R A C T O R : **JOHN TURNER**

M E C H A N I C A L   E N G I N E E R : **JEFFERIES ENGINEERING**

M A S T E R   P L A N   F O R   D E S E R T   H I G H L A N D S : **GAGE DAVIS ASSOCIATES**

IRA'S FOUNTAIN

P O R T L A N D
O R E G O N

At 2:00 in the morning on May 21, 1970, Angela Danadjieva, a small, energetic landscape architect working for Lawrence Halprin's firm, stood in awe above a massive concrete fountain in Portland, Oregon. She herself had designed the irregular, staccato escarpment that stretches eighty feet across the one-acre park, but now, in the harsh glare of the construction lights, the fountain seemed a cyclopean abyss. Eighteen feet below, fountain consultant Dick Chaix was almost ready to turn on the water for the first time. They had chosen this hour for the water test in case it didn't work— better to fail under the cover of night. "By the way," Chaix called up to Danadjieva, "this is the first time I've done a fountain this big."

A low rumble was heard from the mechanical room underneath the concrete walls. Water began to flow from the three sources on the upper level, filling the three-and-a-half-foot-deep pools on top and finally spilling—turbulent and explosive—over the rough surface of the walls. If the fountain had seemed big before, it now seemed very big and very dangerous. Yet Chaix and Danadjieva quickly waded into the upper pools to check the flow over the weirs. Since the opening of the fountain in 1970, thousands have repeated their shallow but dramatic plunge into one of the most exhilarating public plazas in America.[1]

The Baroque fountains of European cities, which also invited people to touch the water, inspired similar civic fountains in America, especially during the City Beautiful movement of the early twentieth century. But their ornamental flourishes and allegorical statues are absent in this Portland park.

The large concrete slabs at the base of the fountain were designed as a stage for both planned and spontaneous performances.

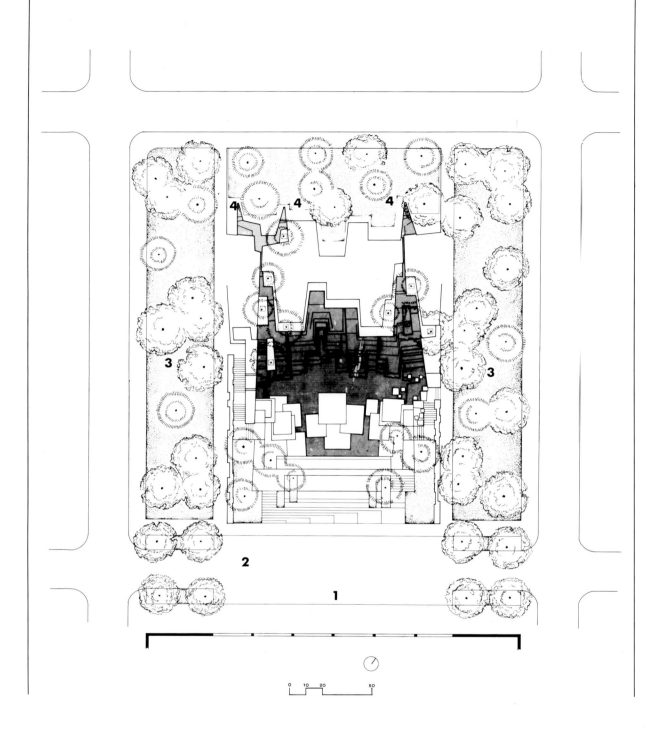

Landscape architect Lawrence Halprin (1916–   ), whose firm designed Ira's Fountain, describes it as the "experiential equivalent" of the cataracts in Oregon's Cascades Mountain Range. The fountain's energy and massive concrete forms also recall the Bonneville Dam and other Columbia River gorge projects. But Ira's Fountain, as the park is called, has its own identity, and this thoroughly modern and American fountain is proudly devoid of iconography, ornamentation, or insipid miniaturizations of nature. It is a sensual pleasure from which one emerges astonishingly refreshed and renewed.

The fountain was designed to *appear* very dangerous but to *be* relatively safe. First-time visitors, unaware of the design's subtle protective features, marvel at the theatrical spectacle of people jumping and clambering on top of the mighty waterfalls. "How can they get away with it? My town would never let us build something like this!"

Portland "got away with it" because of the persuasive powers and salesmanship of Lawrence Halprin. At one point the fountain's present site was to be a parking lot for the new civic auditorium. Halprin convinced the city to create a park instead and to incorporate it into an eight-block open space sequence connecting three major parks. The first, built in 1966, was named Lovejoy Plaza; the second, Pettygrove Park; the third, Auditorium Forecourt— the original name of Ira's Fountain. The names are all emotional correlatives: Lovejoy Plaza is the site of an exuberant fountain, Pettygrove Park is marked by grassy knolls and trees, and Forecourt is a dramatic plaza fronting the auditorium. Together they embody what Halprin believes are the three vital organs of urban life: social, extroverted activity; quiet, peaceful refuge from city crowds; and

ceremonial, theatrical celebration. A healthy city is a matrix of all three activities, and all three can be found to varying degrees in the Portland Open Space Sequence.[2]

Lovejoy Plaza's pinwheeling, cascading waterfall and playful steps were an instant success. Dramatic photographs of people frolicking and sliding through the cascades were a telling critique on the vast, empty plazas American cities were building in imitation of European piazzas. Although Halprin was already well known for his early modern California gardens, plazas, residential complexes, and corporate campuses, Lovejoy thrust him into the public eye as a new breed of landscape architect—one who made parks to climb on, splash in, and revel in. Halprin's office grew as he became engaged in an astonishing range of international projects. Perhaps the most protean landscape architect of his time, Halprin was a tireless proselytizer for revitalizing cities with strong, coordinated open

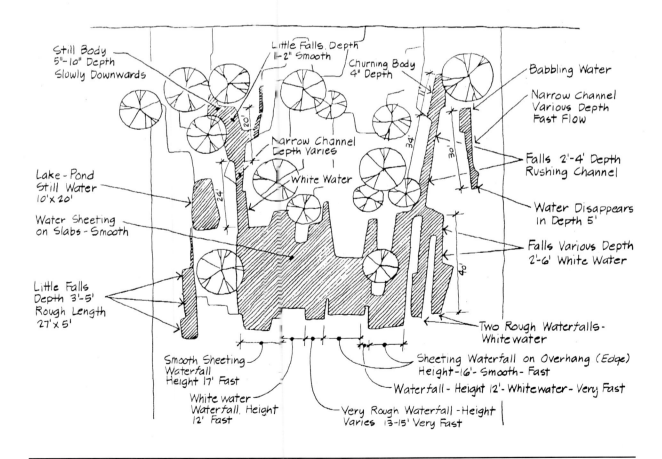

Angela Danadjieva's preliminary sketch of the water effects served as the basis for the engineers' structural and hydraulic plans. Courtesy of Richard Chaix.

space plans. Eager to tap into the late-1960s energy of dissent and innovation, Halprin sought out creative young associates, many of whom came from unorthodox backgrounds.

For the design of Ira's Fountain, Halprin turned to a Bulgarian émigré, Angela Danadjieva (1931–   ). She had designed movie sets in Bulgaria and studied architecture at the Ecole des Beaux-Arts in Paris, and she had come to America after winning, with Ivan Tzvetin, an international competition for the new San Francisco Civic Center Plaza. The plaza was never built, but Danadjieva soon found herself in Halprin's office, and, she recalled, "When everyone else went on vacation, I was supposed to design Ira's Fountain."

All the projects of the Portland Open Space Sequence were designed according to Halprin's theory of the "experiential equivalent of nature." Halprin believed that the form should "come from nature, not on a picturesque level, but on a biological level." For instance, Halprin thought it was folly to try to reproduce the majesty of the Columbia River gorge in a one-acre park, but he was sure that one could create a similar narrative experience. An artificial environment in the city could connect people to the natural environment, not in any pictorial way, but in their visceral reactions to great heights, surging water, rough surfaces, and dense vegetation. Instead of scaling Ira's Fountain to its one-acre site, Halprin wanted to create an independent scale relationship, juxtaposing the people using the plaza with the overwhelming amplitude of mountain cataracts.[3]

Halprin had grown up in Brooklyn and loved the raucous excitement of a thriving metropolis, but Danadjieva, coming from postwar Bulgaria, was shocked at the noise and traffic of American cities. She says, "I didn't even know how to drive, so you can imagine how overwhelming it all was. When I started designing the plaza, all I wanted to do was make the traffic disappear. My design had nothing to do with the High Sierras. It was all environmental mitigation. I used all that water to drown out the traffic."[4]

Danadjieva worked with a clay model instead of drawings, so the fountain evolved as a subtractive

The city can only afford to have the water running about eight hours a day, but the rich texture of the concrete and the cobblestone pavement at the top of the fountain holds one's interest during the "off hours."

Trees are incorporated into the design as sculptural elements. OPPOSITE

volume rather than as an object to be placed in the plaza. This design process enabled her to transform the entire site into a fountain organically. The existing site slopes toward the auditorium and was warped from east to west. Starting with her single block of clay, Danadjieva carved away until she had depressed the plaza enough to separate it from the city traffic. The irregular carvings also served to disguise the site's diagonal slope. At first she envisioned a series of waterfalls, but she later simplified the water sequence to three sources merging into one long waterfall. She continued to carve, and invented more and more ways for people to touch the water. There are water stairs to climb, caves to enter behind the walls, shallow wading pools, concrete blocks for walking across the water without getting wet, and, for the introverted, places to sit apart and watch the show. Danadjieva used calipers to translate the dimensions of the clay

model into design development drawings.

Ira's Fountain's plasticity and continuity of forms distinguish it from the contemporaneous architecture movement known as "Brutalism"—which also used tons of exposed concrete. However, Brutalist architects such as Paul Rudolph made collages of large blocks of concrete around windows, doors, and courtyard spaces, and further individualized the blocks by vertically raking or fluting the exposed concrete. The concrete forms at Ira's Fountain are richly textured and nondirectional so as to bind the different forms together. It has weathered beautifully and appears to have been carved out of an existing block of concrete instead of assembled from different blocks in the Brutalist manner.

Both Danadjieva and Halprin, whose wife, Anna, is an avant-garde dancer and choreographer, wanted the base of the fountain to serve as an

The view of Ira's Fountain
from the Portland Auditorium.

actual performance stage. As it happened, part of Danadjieva's winning entry for the Civic Center Plaza—four overlapping squares—made a perfect figural stage for the base. The water usually runs about eight hours a day, but even without the water, the stage and sculptural forms still sustain attention. Sometimes the fountain is turned off for concerts or other events, and sometimes the water is part of the show: One night, Rudolf Nureyev closed his performance on the auditorium's indoor stage, then spontaneously danced in the fountain.

Danadjieva had planned to enclose the front of the plaza, but Halprin insisted that the stage remain open to the auditorium, especially since the open space sequence leads people between the auditorium and the plaza. Viewed from the auditorium side, with its steps leading down to the "stage," the waterfalls are an effective theatrical backdrop, and at night, when the water is lit, people in front are silhouetted like shadow puppets. The steps and the sidewalk form a direct conceptual connection between the auditorium and the fountain.

Less successful are the other perimeters, whose lack of consistency and resolution is symptomatic of the conflict between Halprin's desire to open the fountain to the city and Danadjieva's wish to offer an asylum from the city. The fountain is shielded on two sides by long berms planted with small flowering trees and some larger maples, and these

have no apparent relationship to the fountain. Too often landscape designers use rows of trees or berms to buffer a park or plaza, as if the berms were a standard picture frame, designed to set off the real subject without attracting attention to itself. Yet in the environment one inhabits the frame. It should be, as the auditorium side of the fountain is, a threshold as well as a buffer, with all the implications of introduction and anticipation.

Civic fountains as original as Ira's Fountain and Lovejoy Plaza are seldom completed without strong civic support. Portland industrialist and philanthropist Ira Keller rallied that support and was instrumental in making sure the plan was not compromised by overly restrictive safety features or other obtrusive additions. In 1978 the city rededicated the fountain to his memory.

Building codes usually require a forty-two-inch barrier—typically a fence or handrail—to protect pedestrians from any sharp drop-off. Ira's Fountain passes code restrictions because each ledge of the eighty-foot-long waterwall includes a forty-two-inch drop behind its two-foot-wide weir, so the weir acts as a parapet, allowing people to splash around in the water without fear of being washed over the edge. Of course, neither the forty-two-inch barrier nor the small signs warning "No swimming or wading allowed" have stopped some Portland youths from performing circus acrobatics along the foun-

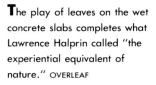

The inscription on the concrete paver reads: IRA'S FOUNTAIN/DEDICATED BY PORTLAND TO IRA KELLER/ "STRENGTH AND BEAUTY COME FROM US—NOT FROM TYRANNY."

The play of leaves on the wet concrete slabs completes what Lawrence Halprin called "the experiential equivalent of nature." OVERLEAF

tain's weirs, much to the delight and amazement of less adventurous souls. The walls are battered outward so that the careless show-off will slide down the slant of the eighteen-foot wall instead of plunging straight down. Another safety factor is that, despite the visual and auditory volume of the water, only one to three inches of water actually flow over the weirs. Fountain consultant Dick Chaix carefully studied different slopes and textures of concrete to achieve the water's illusory force and volume.

An attorney for the Bureau of Risk Management for the City of Portland explains that since the fountain *looks* dangerous, the city is less worried about lawsuits originating from it than from a rusty bolt in a playground swing. "We apply the reasonable person test, meaning that for someone not under the influence of drugs or alcohol [and even most who are] the danger would be very obvious." In over twenty years, the fountain's frolics have never resulted in a significant claim for damages.[5] "Everyone agrees it's worth the risk because it has become such a major landmark for the city."[6]

In its ingenuity and its mechanical power, and in the raw vigor of its forms, Ira's Fountain is a triumph of American engineering—built with the can-do American spirit that harnessed the wild Columbia River and erected the Grand Coulee Dam. Like those dams—which are also popular tourist attractions—the fountain's dense, massive concrete walls strongarm the water into geometrical cataracts. There is formal and spiritual concordance between the WPA and other park projects along the Columbia River and both Lovejoy Plaza and Ira's Fountain; in the recreational areas and scenic overlooks of the Cascades, the straight forms of the stairways are forceful and direct, each one striking out in a slightly different direction down the mountainside. The use of these straight forms was more an economic decision than an aesthetic one; it would have been too costly to make curved steps that would follow the mountains' contours more gracefully. The same is true of the angular forms of Ira's Fountain, which cost $500,000 to build, a very low budget considering its mechanical equipment.[7] This directness of form and economy

of means further distinguish it from the intricately elaborate fountains in European plazas.

There is utility in both the Grand Coulee Dam and Ira's Fountain—one brings electricity to the city, the other brings "electric" relief from the city in a phenomenon known as the Lenard Effect. Running water generates negative ions that counteract the depressant influence of positive ions, which are produced in great quantities by automobiles and other urban pollutants. Thus running water literally helps "wash off" the ills of the city. Danadjieva's mother once told her that whatever she decided to do with her life, she should "be a 'doctor' and help people, heal people." The landscape architect recalls, "I hadn't heard about negative ions, but I knew that running water was good for you."

Built during the peak of the tensions and confrontations of the Vietnam War, Ira's Fountain healed. Hippies flocked to the fountain and, much to the relief of conservative citizens, peacefully "policed" the park themselves. Halprin had worried that people were becoming estranged from life and believed, like Wallace Stevens, that "The greatest poverty is not to live in the physical world."[8] At the fountain's dedication, Halprin sensed that the crowd of politicians, businessmen, and other polite spectators were missing the point, so he kicked off his shoes, rolled up his pants, and went dancing through the pools.

P R O J E C T : **IRA'S FOUNTAIN**

C L I E N T : **PORTLAND DEVELOPMENT COMMISSION**

D A T E O F C O M P L E T I O N : **1970**

L O C A T I O N : **PORTLAND, OREGON**

L A N D S C A P E A R C H I T E C T : **LAWRENCE HALPRIN AND ASSOCIATES**
PROJECT DESIGNER: **ANGELA DANADJIEVA**
PARTNER-IN-CHARGE: **SATORU NISHITA**
PROJECT DIRECTOR: **BYRON McCULLEY**

C O N T R A C T O R : **SCHRADER CONSTRUCTION COMPANY, INC.**

M E C H A N I C A L & E L E C T R I C A L E N G I N E E R S :
BEAMER/WILKINSON ASSOCIATES
SENIOR ASSOCIATE: **RICHARD CHAIX**

What appears to be a massive torrent of water flowing over the edge is actually no more than one to three inches deep.

BECTON DICKINSON

F R A N K L I N   L A K E S
N E W   J E R S E Y

During the 1960s and 1970s, much of the architectural design of American corporate headquarters was directly involved with the efficient organization of the workplace, from the layout of departmental divisions to the configuration of individual work stations. As at CIGNA and Weyerhaeuser, the architecture was an expression of modular systems, *burolandschaft,* or other internal organizational systems. But by the 1980s, as architecture became an increasingly specialized profession, the lead architect often did not even design the work spaces within the building; that task was given over to a firm specializing in space planning and interior design. At the same time, corporations became much more interested in projecting a particular image or style independent of the daily operations of the workplace. At Becton Dickinson Headquarters in Franklin Lakes, New Jersey, the standardized partitioned work stations are efficient, but their functional design is far removed in spirit from the remarkable artistic detailing of the public areas of the building.

Becton Dickinson is a corporate villa: a complex of buildings designed for the use and enjoyment of the company and its guests. As in a classical villa, Becton Dickinson is a locus for ideas about artifice, nature, and arcadian themes of order and decay. While this is clearly a villa of *negotium,* where one comes for business, not relaxation, the complex and the landscape afford Becton Dickinson employees a slow revelation of the design's many pleasures and layers of meaning.

Becton Dickinson is an international supplier

Virginia creeper climbs the rear wall of Building I at Becton Dickinson's headquarters.

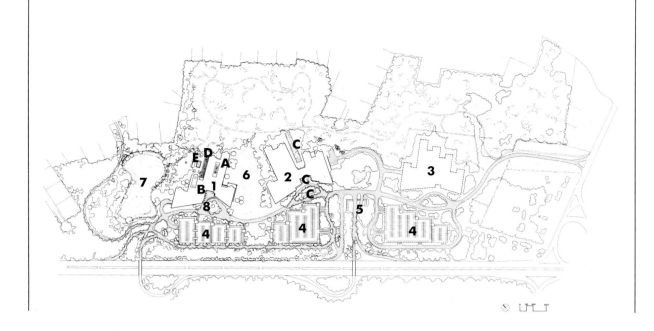

of medical supplies and diagnostic equipment, and its officers did not think it appropriate to build a lavish and grandiose headquarters, as if the company were wealthy at the expense of the ill. At the same time, CEO Wesley Howe and vice-president Dr. Wilson Nolen were architecturally sophisticated clients who wanted their head office to be a consummate example of intelligent architecture, craftsmanship, and art. And although the company did not want to take its place along New Jersey's corporate corridors, such as Route 1 in Princeton, rural communities that had managed to avoid such rapacious development were unwilling to accept Becton Dickinson's one-million-square-foot building program in their own backyard. The company tried unsuccessfully to locate in several different areas before its leaders took a fancy to a wooded 127-acre site in the affluent community of Franklin Lakes.

Becton Dickinson's first priority was to find a landscape architect who could prepare a site plan that would be approved by Franklin Lakes' review boards, and the company chose Morgan Wheelock, Inc., a landscape architecture firm based in Boston. In addition to his firm's commercial projects, Morgan Wheelock (1938–) had designed several prestigious horse farms. "Morgy has style," Nolen explained. "He had won the competition for the Queen's enclosure at Ascot. I thought that would

help put him over with the local gentry."[1]

Wheelock prepared a study of corporate headquarters demonstrating that although raising a building off its site had less impact on the landscape, the people using such a building had less contact with nature. Wheelock's site plan called for three well-grounded buildings blending into the woods, with parking garages and a heavy landscape buffer shielding the complex from the road. This low-keyed concept was instrumental in gaining the approval of local governing boards and community watchdog organizations.

For the area between the first two buildings, Wheelock proposed what is called the "Great Lawn." Earth would be subtracted from the area, so the buildings would appear to have been sited on ridges. This sculpted green bowl would bind the two buildings visually, and its sensuous contours would contrast with the architecture's horizontality and help solve the drainage problem created by the existing undersized storm-water pipes. Water would be collected in the Great Lawn and directed to catch basins in the woods, where it would then be piped to a large retention basin. The three buildings would be built in phases, with the second phase scheduled for completion in 1991.

Wheelock suggested to Becton Dickinson's officers that Kallmann, McKinnell & Wood (KMW), also of Boston, would be the perfect architects for the complex. Wheelock had measured his clients well, for Nolen and his colleagues quickly fell in love with KMW's work, especially admiring the firm's recently completed American Academy of Arts and Science in Cambridge, Massachusetts.

Working with Wheelock, KMW refined the master plan by designing the buildings as long fingers stretching from the parking garage into the woods, thereby maximizing the perimeters for office windows and melding the structures into the landscape.

The architecture is episodic, with projecting wings, towers, atriums, and other discrete elements assembled across the site. Outside, the facades orient the three-story building wings to the landscape—particularly the Great Lawn—with what appear to be French doors but are in fact fixed windows, and by a continuous strip window on the top floor that suggests a studio space instead of individual offices. Michael McKinnell of KMW

The reflecting pool at the entrance to Building I is ringed with sycamore trees.

is particularly pleased with the way "the end of the roof juts forward, engaging the woods, and the final columns stand free in light and air." In the interior, instead of organizing the circulation around the atriums as at CIGNA, the atriums and the views are delightful discoveries.

Gerhard Kallmann (1915–) acknowledges KMW's "preoccupation with certain issues and themes," including the influences of Frank Lloyd Wright, Carlo Scarpa, and Greene and Greene. One of the themes of these architects is the use of nature—vines, mosses, vegetation, and water—to create a dialectical relationship between constructed architectural and landscape forms and the natural process. This dialectic objectifies the struggle between the will to build and the evanescence of what is built. The Becton Dickinson project gave KMW an opportunity for what Michael McKinnell (1935–) described as "the evocative dialogue between the classical and the rude, between order and decay, which was also a theme we explored in the Academy of Science." McKinnell hoped the complex at Becton Dickinson would express "both the order and optimism of the classical spirit and romantic ideas about the ultimate fate of all our work."[2]

Wheelock's site plan is based on this theme. The Great Lawn was designed to be a green valley leading into the dark woods. On the other side of Building I, storm-water runoff is collected in a large detention basin, and a circumferential path invites employees to observe the ebb and flow of water after heavy rains. Nurseryman Kurt Bluemel planted ornamental grasses and hardy perennials in this basin; in the summer, the blooms surge through the basin's eddies and swirls. In winter, the dried stalks of the golden or bleached white grasses remain above the snow.

The same theme is carefully orchestrated at the entrance to Building I. Wheelock planned "an arrival sequence that would introduce visitors to the rural site. Becton Dickinson agreed not to have a covered walkway, so that visitors would walk across the landscape from the parking garage, which gave us an opportunity to design a thematic forecourt."[3] (Though Nolen admits he sometimes wishes there were a tunnel, he reflects that braving the

The first atrium, designed by artist Michael Singer. Becton Dickinson's theme of classical perfection and its inevitable dissolution by natural processes is captured in the juxtaposition of the perfect white columns and the roughness of the stone segments.

The intricate layering of Michael Singer's atrium design suggests an archeological excavation in progress.

flower pots that will accomplish the same task while harmonizing with the rusticated base of the building columns, but these haven't yet been executed.

Once the building was under construction, Becton Dickinson commissioned two artists—Michael Singer (1945–   ) and Richard Fleischner (1944–   )—to develop the atrium spaces. While the artists have distinctly different sensibilities and artistic agendas, both are committed to the same high level of craftsmanship and joining of materials.

Singer's installation for the first atrium, bounded by the three-story columns next to the cafeteria, is an eloquent narrative about the relationship between artifice and its predestined erosion by natural processes. His collage of reflecting pools, water channels, and rough granite blocks contains deep and narrow pits, within whose inaccessible interiors one can glimpse scaffolding and wood braces supporting slabs of granite and pieces of stone. The delicate tendrils of two different ground covers—creeping fig (*Ficus repens*) and creeping Charlie (*Pilea nummulariifolia*)—quietly cover the stones and inch toward the columns. Besides evoking the romantic image of overgrown ruins, the ground covers bind together Singer's complex conceptual and material layering. The Islamic ideal of classical perfection is suggested in the purity of the Moorish pools and runnels and called into question by the off-axis alignment of the square pool. Singer's geometric excavations have an archeological atmosphere, as if the project were exposing the foundations of a previous building on the same site. The granite slabs of the floor render ambiguous whether this new edifice is being built *over* the old or *with* the old, and offer a reminder of the many historical references and precedences found in the rest of the architecture and grounds.

This narrative is subtly elaborated in the smaller second atrium, which faces the cafeteria terrace. At one end, Singer placed a rusted quarry cart loaded with a slab of cleanly sawn granite. At the other end, on a stone podium, is a layered assemblage of wood and stone, which might be taken as a kind of archeological display of construction materials or as a ritualistic offering.

Morgan Wheelock admires the ambiguity and

elements prepares one for the challenges of the day.)

The forecourt is organized around a circular reflecting pool ringed by sycamore trees. Resolving the asymmetrical geometries of the building and the parking garage, the circle evokes a sacred grove, as if the building's angles derived from enclosing and preserving the pool. The bottom of the pool is covered with wide slabs of granite, and the drains and mechanical devices are concealed beneath the seams of the granite slabs. Like much of the landscape detailing at Becton Dickinson, the pool is both exquisite and difficult to maintain—crews must diligently vacuum sycamore leaves and other droppings out of the pool before these clog the filters. Working with KMW, Wheelock designed the paving to radiate from the pool to the entrance, gradually metamorphosing from a rough texture to smoother pavers to the granite sets of the vehicular drop-off, and finally to the steps and the entrance to the building. Ironically, the steps blend so perfectly into the pavement that visitors occasionally tripped on them, so now terra-cotta pots mark the place where the steps merge into the grade of the granite sets. Wheelock has designed low stone poetic resonance of Singer's work. His associate Andrew Leonard, who was the project manager for the Becton Dickinson headquarters, remarked on the differences between the landscape architect's design process and Singer's: "As landscape architects we are much more resolved in our approach to design, and I think that our forecourt and Michael's atrium work wonderfully together because they apply different sensibilities or artistic processes to similar themes. Both the atrium and the forecourt use still water and circular pools as well as the same material, so the project feels like they belong in the same place."[4] For Building II, Singer will design both the forecourt and the outdoor space between the two projecting wings of the building, and one will be able to explore the different levels of Singer's design as it steps down the slope toward the woods. Singer plans to restate the themes of the first atrium, only in a more spatial design. He explains: "Vines will grow up the enclosing walls and into the piece so there won't be a clear separation between the building and the granite. Water will begin near the building and work its way down the slope until it seems to disappear into the woods."[5]

Environmental artist Richard Fleischner was originally commissioned to design a piece for one of the two atriums, but he asked to design the cafeteria terrace and environs instead. Even though the terrace had already been designed and the paving material purchased, Becton Dickinson and Morgan Wheelock agreed to accept Fleischner's proposal if he used the same paving material.

In his previous work, Fleischner had been concerned with movement and physical orientation as a means of learning about a specific place and had utilized geometrical suggestions of gate, floor, and furniture to bring a sense of human occupation and order to a forest's rambling growth patterns. Wheelock's original design had brought the woods up to the cafeteria terrace, but Fleischner thought that the area needed more spatial definition to encourage people to circulate and explore the woods. Fleischner also felt that allowing the woods to come up to the terrace would create too sharp a demarcation between nature and artifice. Instead,

In the foreground of the second atrium an old quarry cart hauls a slab of granite. At the other end an assemblage of wood and stone rests on a stone podium. OPPOSITE

The terrace, designed by Richard Fleischner, is punctuated with beds of dropmore purple (*Lythrum salicaria*). ABOVE

The paving pattern and perennial flower beds of the terrace mediate between the hard walls of the building and the New Jersey woods. RIGHT

he calibrated and clarified the site in terms of boundaries, tree canopies, and junctions between paved areas, lawn, and meadows to provide a harmonious interaction between nature and culture so that the interventions neither tame the site nor deny the psychological comfort of orientation.

Fleischner patterned the terrace using the purchased square granite paving material, punctuated with perennial flower beds, and oriented with teak benches. From the terrace he layered the site toward the woods. The perennial beds present tall, robust flowers including daylilies, fall asters, lythrum, and phlox. The next layer is a wildflower meadow, with a twenty-five by fifty-foot sunken lawn panel on axis with the circular stairwell; the edge of the meadow and woods is marked by a line of birch trees. The trees were designed to "lead into the woods," but birches need sunlight and the first planting fared badly, so the trees are to be replanted after thinning the forest canopy. The implied rectangle that is formed, on two sides, by

the building is reinforced by teak benches and screens in the manner of Scottish architect Charles Mackintosh (1868–1928). Mackintosh's distinctive furniture and interior detailing—small square patterns either in an open lattice or inlaid on wide boards—was also employed by KMW for the interior handrails, cafeteria booths, and room dividers. Further into the woods, Fleischner sited a granite bench and settee on a square plinth, which one comes across as casually as one discovers the remnants of stone fences elsewhere on the property. The isolation of the carefully crafted granite plinth as the leaves quietly settle on it continues the dialogue between the classical and romantic. Fleischner also planned a rectangular opening in the woods as an analog to the atriums, but this has not been constructed.

Fleischner prefers on-site judgments over design conferences. Like many artists who work directly with materials or full-scale models instead of drawings, Fleischner had difficulties coordinating with Morgan Wheelock's office. Well before a site is even cleared, landscape architects have to make carefully detailed plans for the contractor to bid

on—a process that is anathema to Fleischner's "hands-on" philosophy. "What works in a drawing doesn't always work on the ground," he says. "A straight line might look best in plan, but a slight curve might work better on uneven ground."[6] Morgan Wheelock commented ruefully, "I admire him. I wish I could spend as much time [as Fleischner does] on the site, but landscape architects can't always work that way and still make a living."[7]

Becton Dickinson has continued to develop the site. Morgan Wheelock designed a series of walking or jogging paths that lead through the different microclimates and topography of the site; these trails are also planned to provide future opportunities for other environmental artists. In the immediate vicinity of the building, however, Becton Dickinson's maintenance has weakened some of the original concept. There is far more lawn area than Wheelock intended—instead of letting an understory develop at the edge of the woods, there is a clear distinction between the lawn and the forest, giving the landscape a more suburban aspect. Nor have the executives been comfortable with Fleischner's wildflower meadow. Jim McCulloch, the land-

Fleischner's layered design for the rear of the building explores the differences between the highly controlled realm of the building, the natural landscape, and all the stages in between. The terrace (left) leads into the cafeteria.

scape coordinator for Becton Dickinson, explains that they felt the original planting's height and wildness were more appropriate for the detention basin than for the cafeteria terrace, and says, "We're going to try some different grasses that can be cut at about four or five inches to give a sense of meadow without being such a contrast with the mowed lawn."[8]

The struggle to construct and maintain an accurate balance between the lawn and meadow or between the shade trees and woods mirrors the ambivalence in Becton Dickinson's longing for the grace and manners of a country house and the plain fact that people come there to work, not to engage in contemplation or casual conversation. There is no place to sit and linger in the grove of sycamores at the forecourt; Singer's atriums are contemplative gardens, but there are no benches or comfortable seating steps—the works are viewed only *en passant*; and Fleischner's benches with their gridded rigidity—both their placement and their perpendicular backs—do not encourage casual camaraderie. As at most modern corporations, employees are far more likely to walk or jog through the landscape than to sit quietly within it.

The architecture and landscape design of Becton Dickinson frame the austerity and independence of the New England spirit, which does not seek solutions in a crowd. Through the year, one observes the expansive solitude of the Great Lawn, the slow embrace of the tender green vines on Singer's excavations, the autumn leaves collecting on Fleischner's granite bench, and countless other poetic evocations of the passage of time.

PROJECT: **BECTON DICKINSON & COMPANY HEADQUARTERS**

CLIENT: **BECTON DICKINSON & COMPANY**

DATE OF COMPLETION: **PHASE ONE: 1987**

LOCATION: **FRANKLIN LAKES, NEW JERSEY**

ARCHITECT: **KALLMANN, McKINNELL & WOOD, ARCHITECTS, INC.**
PRINCIPALS-IN-CHARGE: **MICHAEL McKINNELL, GERHARD KALLMANN, HENRY WOOD**

LANDSCAPE ARCHITECT: **MORGAN WHEELOCK, INC.**
PRINCIPAL-IN-CHARGE: **MORGAN WHEELOCK**
PROJECT MANAGER: **ANDREW LEONARD**
PROJECT TEAM: **CAROL TRANSKI, TRUDI MILLER LAVIGNE, ROBERT WOODBURN, JOHN AMODEO, EDWARD MARSHALL**

ARTISTS: **MICHAEL SINGER, RICHARD FLEISCHNER**

WET MEADOW DESIGN: **KURT BLUEMEL, INC.**

CIVIL ENGINEER: **ANDREW MARSHALL**

STRUCTURAL ENGINEERS: **ZALDASTANI ASSOCIATES, INC.**

MECHANICAL ENGINEERS: **COSENTINI ASSOCIATES**

FOUNTAIN CONSULTANT: **CMS COLLABORATIVE**

LANDSCAPE CONTRACTORS: SITE WORK: **HENDERSON CORPORATION**
LANDSCAPING: **ROCKLEDGE GARDEN CENTER**

THE DONNELL GARDEN

S O N O M A
C A L I F O R N I A

Most landscape architecture historians agree that the Donnell Garden in Sonoma, California, designed by Thomas D. Church, is the most famous modern American private garden. It is indisputably the most photographed garden and the first shots of its swimming pool appeared in *House Beautiful* so soon after it was finished in 1948 that the magazine colored in the unplanted lawn.

The swimming pool—the house itself was seldom pictured—became an icon of good modern design: a wooden deck, simple steel chairs, and a modern abstract sculpture as a gentle focal point. Looking at the photos, one could almost feel the chlorinated water and the suntan lotion, smell the hamburgers cooking on the grill, and taste a daiquiri from the wet bar in the pool house. Its sensual modernity is much closer to Matisse than to Mies. Academics have published scholarly articles about the Donnell Garden, analyzing the influence of cubism, surrealism, and other modern art movements, debating the source of the free-form pool, and carefully diagramming the garden's overlapping planes, multiple axes, and transparencies. Even after "kidney-shaped pools" became a California cliché, the Donnell Garden was still held to be a modern masterpiece.

Given the fame of the Donnell Garden, one might expect it to be the avatar of Church's lifelong explorations. Instead, it is something of an anomaly. In his book *Gardens Are For People*, published seven years after the garden's completion, only three out of fifteen swimming pools were free-form.

The Donnell pool's curvilinear shape is echoed by Adaline Kent's undulating sculpture.

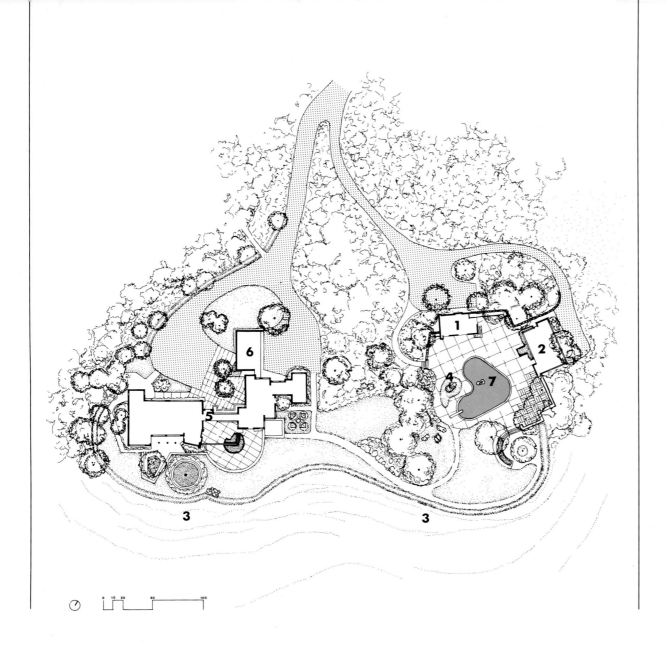

By the time Church wrote *Your Private Garden* in 1969, the Donnell was the only non-rectilinear design of the fourteen swimming pools included. Yet in each of Church's books, the Donnell Garden was favored with the most photographs and drawings. It stood out—capturing the public imagination and the spirit of its time—and it epitomized all the lessons of clean, unpretentious design that Church had patiently advocated in writing and in his professional practice throughout his life.

The Donnell Garden is built on a ranch north of San Francisco. Before World War II the Bay Area's landscape was primarily comprised of dairy farms and vineyards, but after the war, newcomers flooded into the area. The region promised "the good life"—a mild climate, no insects, and a long dry season—and with a little irrigation, anything would grow.

Many of the newcomers, weary of wartime frugality, wanted new, up-to-date houses. Younger architects and landscape architects seized the opportunity to experiment with new styles, materials, and techniques. Their designs revealed a prevailing Japanese influence of wood construction, simplicity, and openness. Instead of traditional houses—the Cape Codders and other starter-home styles on the East Coast—Bay Area newcomers wanted smaller, more affordable houses that were clean, honest,

A pasture on the Donnell ranch, El Novillero. The owners chose a thick grove of live oaks as the site for the house and pool. LEFT

The approach to the house takes visitors through a landscape of rolling grassland. BELOW

and functional, with all the modern conveniences. Unpretentious industrial materials were combined with redwood construction.

Thomas Church (1902–1978) set up practice in California in 1929. He had been educated at Harvard's Graduate School of Design and had traveled widely, but to his many clients, he was "Tommy," an ingenious and good-humored garden designer. Friends and clients who watched Church sketch out their garden design on some note paper might have been unaware of the knowledge and sophistication that lay behind the seemingly effortless designs—one is reminded of the Zen master who, when asked how long he had taken to complete a brush painting, replied, "Seventy years and one minute. Seventy years to learn how to do it and one minute to do it." Church soon became very well known, thanks to *Sunset* magazine and, especially, *House Beautiful,* which published a Church garden in every issue for eight years. Scholars estimate that he designed over two thousand gardens during his long career.

Church's popular books celebrated the sunshine, joy, and bourgeois hedonism of the postwar era. He emphasized simple lessons in organization for a generation coping with its baby boom: "The playpen and sandbox should be visible from both the kitchen and living room. . . . If the garden of today sounds like a three-ring circus, remember that it is a complete universe in itself and must provide for every aspect of family living."[1]

Unlike Garrett Eckbo or James Rose, other landscape architects who published extensively during the post–World War II era, Church was not interested in promoting modern materials, such as aluminum and plastics, or even, necessarily, modern design. His own work ranged from asymmetric, constructivist compositions to serene, unapologetic, symmetrical classicism. These gardens were designed for the clients who would use them, not for Church's own artistic explorations or social statements. His designs profess their limitations so candidly that it hardly seems proper to note their lack of intensity or ambition; there is joy in the simple facts of these gardens' existence and in their owners' heartfelt appreciation.

A gently curving path, bordered by a flowing hedge, connects the pool to the house. OPPOSITE

From the house, a bank of shrubs and flowers masks the pool, while the long, curving hedge defines the horizon of the plateau on which the house and pool are built.

Church's small office was an important training ground for the postwar generation of landscape architects, including Lawrence Halprin, Robert Royston, and Doug Baylis. The large number of quickly constructed projects that came through the office enabled these young designers to experiment with new forms. The early 1950s provided little public, corporate, or institutional work for landscape architects, but as the economic climate improved, many of Church's "graduates" went on to build large corporate practices. Church himself served as consultant on some larger projects, but his office remained small and dedicated to the expression of democratic humanism. In *Gardens Are For People* he wrote: "What you will have, I hope, is a garden

more beautiful than you had anticipated, with less care than you had expected, and costing only a little more than you had planned."[2]

The Donnell Garden began simply enough when Dewey and Jean Donnell decided to build a house on their ranch, "El Novillero," in the Sonoma hills. The site they had chosen for the house lay in a grove of live oaks on a plateau overlooking a meandering salt marsh and San Pablo Bay in the distance. It is approached through dry, rolling grassland, which is in vivid contrast to the now even more verdant house and pool complex.

The Donnells asked Church to design their pool complex before the house was built, and he selected a small knoll just up from where the house

The arbor next to the house is covered with a cat-claw vine (*Macfadyena unguiscati*), which is native to the West Indies.

was to be. George Rockrise, a young designer in Church's office, designed the pool house, and Lawrence Halprin refined the construction details. The lanai, though designed by Rockrise at the same time, was not built until 1951. The main house, built in 1952, is connected to the pool by a sweeping asphalt path. Church and architect Austin Pierpont worked closely together to unite the house and its terraces and to preserve existing live oaks. Church also designed a geometrical herb parterre near the kitchen, a charming example of his unpretentious eclecticism.

Working from a printed survey of the knoll, Church determined that there was not enough level ground for a comfortable pool complex and decided to extend the horizontal surface instead of using steps and different levels to fit the design into the existing topography. Church didn't use this method for all his designs; he reserved it for projects like the Donnell pool complex, which he felt would be weakened if it were not all on the same level. For the Donnell pool, this meant extending a wood deck over the hillside on the south side in order to allow a generous pool area and to include a small grove of live oaks within the pool plateau. The lanai was placed at an angle to the grid of the pool house and deck in order not to cut further into the hillside. Once the dimensions of the wooden deck and lanai were calculated, the undulant curves for the swimming pool and its companion planting bed completed the necessary elements.

Church made some bird's-eye perspective drawings and some rough plans. These sketches clearly show the axial organization of the garden. The sixty-foot-long pool is basically a "dog-leg," creating a shallow end for children and a deep end with diving board for grown-ups. A primary axis is created by the angling of the lanai: instead of directly facing the pool's central sculpture—which it would do if it were located on the concrete grid—it is turned to confront a space between the sculpture and the island planting. The lanai's long view is framed by the live oaks just beyond the pool.[3]

The garden's evolution from Church's sketch

The Donnell pool's sensuous shape and inviting coolness contrast sharply with the dry grassland of the ranch.

to its actual construction, supervised by Lawrence Halprin, reveals the kind of precise design changes that belied Church's seemingly casual process. Originally, both the pool and the outline of the concrete deck were designed with compound curves. During construction, however, the concrete was formed with radial curves whose sharpness make the pool seem more relaxed. On paper, the planting island was a rather amorphous amoebic shape. When it was constructed, its configuration was sharpened and visually locked into the outline of the swimming pool.

Another important change was the substitution of the commissioned sculpture by Adaline Kent for the boulder shown in Church's original sketch. The landscape architect, in his typical nonchalant fashion, explained that the boulder was too rough and that Kent's sculpture had a playful opening underwater. Furthermore, one could dive from the top of the sculpture or use its concave surface for sunbathing.

Church said that the forms of the pool and the deck were inspired by the winding salt marshes below, and even though the undulating patterns are visually analogous, Church's explanation was made ex post facto. The Donnells never remembered Church mentioning the salt marsh as an inspiration for the shape of the pool.[4] The idea first appeared in the House Beautiful article by Mary Roche (the first publication of the Donnell Garden), and Church may have liked it enough to use it in his book. Church's designs seldom mimicked natural forms beyond the site, and the shape is very similar to a grass island in a concrete grid he had designed two years earlier for the Menefee Garden in the Oregon woods.

However, scholars have advanced many interpretations and possible sources of inspiration for the Donnell Garden. It shares a formal affinity with surrealist artwork, particularly the biomorphic abstractions of Jean Arp and Juan Miró. Church's impish explanation for the Kent sculpture reveals his sympathy for the playful mood of the early surrealists. Though surrealism later became identified with dream-inspired imagery and alienation, the term was first used by French poet Guillaume

Apollinaire in a 1917 review of ballet decor by Picasso: "a sort of sur-realism . . . promises to transform arts and manners from top to bottom with universal joy."

Alvar Aalto's curvilinear forms have also been proposed as an important influence, especially since Church had visited Aalto in 1937, and he and his wife opened a showroom for Aalto furniture in San Francisco in 1939. Church had a facility for domesticating artistic forms and may have simply thought that given the right site conditions, Aalto's free-form shapes for vases and furniture would translate well into landscape forms. At any rate, the Donnell Garden's references to surrealist art or Aalto furniture gave its design an artistic authority that was lacking in Church's more symmetrical gardens. Its biomorphic forms and sculpture became an icon of intellectual status that today's generation might call a "designer label."

Of course, if the Donnell pool did not possess such formal authority, there would be little interest in these speculations. The pool is both convex and concave—the concavity a seeming deformation caused by the grass island, whose two large boulders give added visual weight to the compressive action of the island. The concavity is balanced by Kent's sculpture in the center of the pool. The convex sides of the pool bulge past the grass island, but are stopped on one side by the lanai and on the other by the diving board. These dynamic relationships can be "read" from the plan view, but one has to swim in the pool to truly appreciate the kinesthetic experience of Church's sculptural expression. Kent's sculpture takes on another dimension from inside the pool—its cavity frames a view of the large rocks on the grass island and its undulating forms are revealed as a quick contour sketch of the tops of the live oaks. When one is submerged in the

The pool and the lanai, seen through the live oaks that punctuate the wooden deck.

Near the pool house, wisteria overhangs a planting of bird of paradise (*Euphorbia niciciana*). The plantlike rods on the right are actually a kinetic metal sculpture.

pool, the trunks of the live oaks are no longer visible, so one seems to be floating among the tree tops. The aquatic experience of the Donnell pool is demonstrable proof that in landscape design the swimming pool is the most intimate nexus of nature and art. The pool itself is complete artifice and the most figural element in a landscape composition, but it is also undeniably experiential—one plunges into the natural element that constitutes sixty percent of the human body.

The garden's plantings are colorful and eclectic, including annuals and popular exotics such as bird of paradise and Japanese aralia. Lawrence Halprin was responsible for some of the horticultural details, such as extending the flower bed at the corner of the lanai to meet the pool's concrete grid, thereby continuing the theme of overlapping forms.

Time and space are different at the Donnell Garden, a slow narrative without the urgency of seasons and vivid contrasts. There are no moral overtones, no obvious references to past cultures. It is a garden on the edge of history, in a climate that is foggy one day and clear and cool the next. Here Church answered the challenge of modern landscape architecture, which was, in Lawrence Halprin's words, "not to make the garden look natural, but to make the garden so the people in it will feel natural."

PROJECT: **PRIVATE RESIDENCE**

DATE OF COMPLETION: **1949**

LOCATION: **SONOMA COUNTY, CALIFORNIA**

LANDSCAPE ARCHITECT: **THOMAS D. CHURCH**
　　　　　　　　　　　　　LEAD DESIGNER: **LAWRENCE HALPRIN**

ARCHITECT: POOL HOUSE, LANAI: **GEORGE ROCKRISE**
　　　　　　　　MAIN HOUSE: **AUSTIN PIERPONT**

SCULPTOR: **ADALINE KENT**

THE CROSBY ARBORETUM

PICAYUNE MISSISSIPPI

The thin, acid soil of the Piney Woods, an area of about 13,000 square miles in southern Mississippi, is best suited for timber and livestock, not for row crops, cotton, sugar cane, or strawberries, all of which were once advanced as possible uses for the stump-dotted wastelands left by turn-of-the-century timber barons. Historian John Napier wrote of the Piney Woods: "One sees irony in that the land has returned to producing timber and livestock, the two products our land yielded so generously to our pioneer ancestors."[1]

In 1979 the Crosby Arboretum began to cultivate the beauty that was often overlooked by lumbermen seeking only profit from this land. By rooting itself firmly in its native soil, the Arboretum now offers a poetic resistance to the gradual assimilation of southern Mississippi into the culture of interstate highways, fast food franchises, and air conditioning. Landscape architect Edward Blake, Jr. (1947–   ), one of the planners of the Arboretum, wants to enhance the people's perception of their own environment: "We live in a garden called Mississippi. We're preserving, in a scientific and artistic way, the best examples of this garden for future generations. Too many people just take all this for granted."[2] The Crosby Arboretum celebrates its region and echoes Wallace Stevens's call for a uniquely American poetry freed from European aestheticism:

The man in Georgia waking among pines
Should be pine-spokesman. The responsive man,

Slash pines (*Pinus elliottii* Engelm) and longleaf pines (*Pinus palustris*) flourish in the Crosby Arboretum's savanna exhibit.

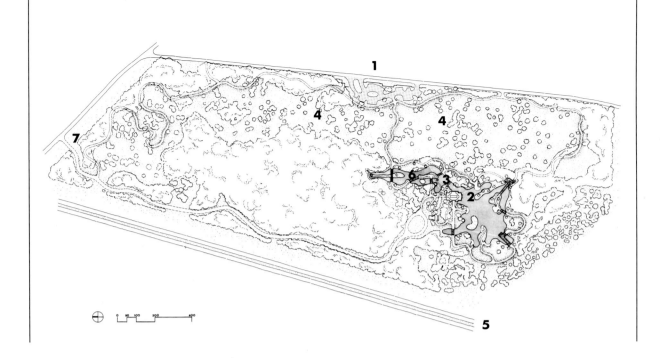

Planting his pristine cores in Florida
Should prick thereof, not on the psaltery,
But on the banjo's categorical gut.[3]

Historically, the Piney Woods has been snubbed as a backwater region of no particular distinction. Columnist and author James J. Kilpatrick wrote of Picayune, the town closest to the Crosby Arboretum: "This is the Deep South . . . scrub pines and flat fields. . . . The land is home to some wealthy professionals and some prosperous merchants, but mostly it is home to po' whites and po' blacks . . . just making do."[4]

Like many small southern towns, Picayune was dominated by a few powerful families, the most prominent being that of timberman Lucius Osmond Crosby (1869–1948). In 1916 Crosby bought 42,000 acres of mostly virgin forest dominated by towering longleaf pines (*Pinus palustris*), and soon controlled production from the tree to the factory—most of the lumber products were shipped to International Harvester in Chicago for farm implements. Reforestation was seldom practiced because few could see the value of waiting 150 years for the trees to mature (modern scientific reforestation has considerably shortened the maturation time) and because the state of Mississippi's ad valorem taxes on standing timber of any size—designed to encourage farming—discouraged reforestation. By the 1920s the timber boom had exhausted the once vast pine forests. At a time when the redwoods of the western United States were being saved for future generations, the Mississippi pines had no champions. One Arboretum board member says that his family hired an artist from New York to paint a remnant of the dense forest of giant virgin pine trees that once covered the land, but never thought to preserve the trees themselves.

By the time the Great Depression set in, the large lumber mills had closed, leaving desolate stumps and scrubby brush strewn across the flat landscape. Crosby, like many Southern leaders, was staunchly anti-union but felt a paternalistic responsibility for his workers, and he tried to find new crops for the land that would provide employment for the men who had worked in his lumber mills and logging camps. Without his leadership and perseverance, Picayune might not have survived until the end of World War II, when new industry, including tung-oil plants and later a major NASA facility, revitalized the economy. Eventually, Crosby's three sons all went into various branches of the family's business. L. O. Crosby, Jr.'s first job out of college in 1936 was overseeing a strawberry farm near Picayune—part of his father's relief effort—on what is now the site of Pinecote,[5] the Crosby Arboretum's Interpretive Center.

The strawberries did not prove to be a viable crop and when the ad valorem tax on standing timber was repealed in 1940, the land was replanted with slash pines (*Pinus elliotti* Engelm). These trees were managed with controlled burns until 1969, when Hurricane Camille ravaged them and the property was abandoned.

Following World War II, L. O. Crosby, Jr., reorganized the family operations and was very active in the community. After his death in 1978, his children decided to found an arboretum as a fitting memorial to a man who loved his native woods and fields and they donated the sixty-four-acre former strawberry farm, which is located fifty miles from New Orleans on Interstate 59.

L. O. Crosby's granddaughter, Lynn Gammill, and the other directors of the Crosby Arboretum, chose not to emulate arboretums whose collections of exotic plants and Japanese gardens re-create a geography of the past or of distant lands. Nor were they pleased with arboretums whose native plant displays are either exhibited side by side without any logical connection between them or isolated like islands surrounded by traditional horticultural displays. Instead they chose the much more profound and difficult task of giving expression to a new vision of the Piney Woods.

Because sixty-four acres is extremely small for an arboretum, the Crosbys decided to enlarge it by including a network of eleven noncontiguous native habitats totaling over 1,700 acres (it is almost impossible to visit the entire Arboretum in a single day). These habitats range in size from forty to 640 acres and are all located within a sixty-mile radius of Pincecote, the Arboretum's most intensively developed area. Pinecote itself is dedicated to public education and plant display, while the eleven natural habitats (more may be added) remain largely undisturbed except for minimal facilities for visitors and scientific study. Visitors come to Pinecote and, having learned about the native habitats, they may drive twenty miles to see a beech/magnolia forest or a typical Piney Woods swamp. At present,

these natural areas are the subject of scientific experiments, such as ecological population studies, and are becoming an invaluable regional resource, but in the early 1980s, the most pressing need of the Crosby Arboretum was the planning and construction of Pinecote.

Landscape architect Ed Blake, a native Mississippian then teaching at Mississippi State University, and the firm of Andropogon Associates, Ltd., Philadelphia, were commissioned to develop a master plan for Pinecote. Landscape architect Carol Franklin of Andropogon notes that "The property had been abandoned after the hurricane and there was very little diversity and almost no aesthetic or scientific merit."[6] Working with scientists from Mississippi State University, the landscape architects determined that the long, flat site could sustain only a small percentage of the ecosystems of the lower Pearl River Basin—the major watershed of the region—without considerable site manipulation. However, this restriction offered an opportunity to design the entire site as a coherent unit, maximizing diversity by stretching the plant displays slightly beyond strict scientific accuracy, but excluding plants that would *never* occur naturally on the sixty-four-acre site.

The ecology of the Piney Woods is subtly complex, and even small changes in topography have powerful ramifications. Because of the high water table, a grade change of a single foot is the ecological equivalent of a hundred feet in New England. The subtle patterns and occurrences of the area's slightly different ecosystems can be as inscrutable for natives as they are for tourists.

The sixty-four acres of Pinecote, a roughly rectangular site, offer several loop trail systems designed to introduce visitors to over sixty small habitats. At the present time, only the Pinecote Pavilion—an open-air shelter—has been constructed, but other pavilions for visitor information and indoor exhibitions are planned. After parking their cars, visitors enter near the center of the site and find themselves in the midst of the savanna exhibit, a fire-controlled pine landscape running parallel to the boundary of the site. From there they can walk to the Pinecote Pavilion, which is

The Pinecote Pavilion at sunset.

used for lectures, poetry readings, and other events, as well as for shelter, and onto the loop path around the two-and-a-half-acre pond. The other major path system begins near the parking lot and runs north through the savanna and the different woodland succession areas in the north-central part of the site.

The decision to create the pond was the most dramatic intervention on the site. Such ponds are rare in the region, but as the Arboretum's staff explains, a pond might have existed on the site if a small stream had been present and been dammed by a farmer or beaver. The Arboretum took advantage of the existing drainage patterns created by an old roadway and the irrigation ditches for the strawberry farm, which ran east to west. The roadway was dug out to become a slough and collect water from the rest of the site. For the first few years, extra water was supplied from an artesian well in order to flush out nutrients that would have promoted excessive algae growth.[7] The Arboretum then built a small dam to mimic the water fluctuations of a typical beaver pond. It was thought that the water level of the pond would fluctuate by two to three feet a year, but the site's perched water table—there is a thick layer of clay only six feet underground—keeps the pond from lowering more than twelve inches. This is sufficient to expose the mud flats around the cypress and tupelo trees—showing the effect of natural fluctuations—without affecting the reflective qualities of the water.

The shape and depth of the pond were carefully designed by Andropogon Associates and Blake to form a picturesque stroll garden,[8] which introduces and isolates different plant communities and offers framed views of the pavilion. Unlike most man-made ponds in the region, which are designed to inhibit the aging process, the pond at Pinecote is designed to work with the aging process. Knowing to what depth a water plant will colonize allowed the designers to minimize maintenance and still control the visual quality and the rhythm of the path system around the pond. Beech trees and cypress trees are planted in places where they might have seeded naturally in a few decades, so the planting plan is designed to push the ecological

succession into high gear, not to create a carefully composed landscape that faces only maintenance or decay.

What is most significant about the design of the Crosby Arboretum is not the plants that exist at any given moment, but the moment itself in the continually evolving landscape. Like a natural pond, Pinecote's pond will change over the years. The amount of aquatic vegetation will increase, and as the adjoining trees shed their leaves or lose branches, they will add to the pond's biomass. Then, as the biomass of the pond increases, trees will grow in the shallows and *their* shedding leaves will encourage more water plants. However, as trees mature and shade the pond, the decreasing sunlight will cause the aquatic plants to die back and the amount of open water will begin to increase. In less than a hundred years, the Pinecote Pavilion will look onto a small body of dark water surrounded by tall cypresses, backed by oaks, tupelos, and hickories.

The ecosystems of the northern part of Pinecote are handled with a confident, broad brush and without the micromanagement of the areas around the pond. Especially compelling is the view of the grasses, which flourish in the open, fire-controlled savanna, against the density of the beech/magnolia forest. Unfortunately, the loopy path system is self-consciously serpentine, while the natural inclination in the flat, open savanna is to walk straight ahead. The noise from Interstate 59, only faintly audible from the pavilion, is distracting, but the Crosby Arboretum is reluctant to construct a sound barrier, because such a solid structure would visually disrupt the long horizon of the savanna.

The ecological planning and architecture at Pinecote are consistent in concept and execution. The soil that was excavated to create the lake was hauled off the site instead of being used, as at the Bloedel Reserve, to create berms or mounds, because such forms are not part of the natural landscape of the Piney Woods. The architect for the Crosby Arboretum, Fay Jones (1921–   ), remarked that it was the first time he had ever seen fill hauled away.

This fidelity to ecological processes characterizes all the work of Andropogon Associates—an

interdisciplinary firm formed in 1975 by four land-scape architects and architects. The firm's name comes from a common broomsedge, which is one of the first grasses to volunteer on disturbed sites or abandoned fields. It reflects the firm's commit-ment to offer economical and environmentally sound alternatives to traditional landscape maintenance. Three of the four founding partners had worked for Ian McHarg, whose book *Design with Nature* (1969) is this century's most influential landscape architec-ture publication. At the time a lonely prophet of environmentalism, McHarg despaired of finding a

publisher for the book, but since its publication it has sold over 200,000 copies.

McHarg's writings stress where to build and how much to build but not what to build. Andro-pogon shares McHarg's allegiance to hard, meas-urable facts, but contends that without an artistic appreciation of pattern, the resulting design may be ecologically sound but uninspiring. Andropogon principal Carol Franklin explains that "Fidelity to the truths of both art and science can be achieved by a fidelity to *pattern*, which is common to both art and science and is both observable and quan-

Delicate aquatic plants at twilight.

The aquatic vegetation in the pond progresses from rooted plants close to the shore to lily pads near the Pavilion.
OPPOSITE

tifiable. . . . For art to reflect accurately the latest, best, scientific information, it requires scientific information that is translated or translatable into PATTERN."[9]

Andropogon demonstrates to clients how ecological site management with native plants, natural hydrologic patterns, and plant succession can achieve a higher degree of stability at lower construction and maintenance costs. The firm's emphasis on the dangers of environmental desecration gives its design exegesis an apocalyptic zeal that was common among nineteenth-century landscape architects such as Frederick Law Olmsted, but that has been missing from the seemingly less emotional modern practitioners. Carol Franklin insists: "We don't have time to debate about styles, about fashions. They are irrelevant to the survival of the diversity of life on our planet. . . . Passion should come first in putting systems back together, reconnecting us spiritually and functionally to the earth."[10]

Ecology is a young science—its first American textbook was published in 1900. Early ecologists described holistic patterns that lead to climax conditions, such as the virgin pine forests of prehistoric Mississippi. In the second half of the twentieth century, ecologists have recognized that the spatial boundaries of ecosystems are seldom clearly delineated and that their spaces interpenetrate, depending on local conditions such as storms or fires (such disturbances were considered by "classical" ecologists to be "noise" that had to be ignored in order to discover universal ecological models). Ecologists have also turned their attention to ecological patterns found in suburban and urban environments.

An understanding of the fragile interdependencies of natural systems has great resonance in a region that is seeking to overcome its traditional hierarchical economic structure, its reliance on rugged individualism, and its often bitter resistance to perceived threats to the local way of life. There is a spiritual correspondence between the Arboretum's stated purpose of engendering "the broader context of man's perception and use of the natural world and the interconnections between the plant world and human lives"[11] and a talk given by economist Dr. Jesse White in 1988, in which he proclaimed that " 'New Souths' have dragged behind them, like long, old chains, the inevitable outcomes of . . . sharecropping, low-wage factories, and segregation. . . . But, something else has become clear—a sense of interdependence . . . a growing awareness that in today's world the good life of one individual is inextricably linked to the good life of the next. The South is part of a complex interdependent nation and a shrinking world."[12]

One of the major connections between humans and the natural world in the Piney Woods is fire—whether controlled or naturally occurring. Ecologist Sidney McDaniel has described the Piney Woods as a region of "complex vegetation under the influence of fire." Before white settlers appeared, fire had been used by the indigenous Indian population to encourage new grass for game. Under the shade of the 120-foot-high yellow pines, wild oats would grow to three or four feet.

In order to give visitors an understanding of man's role in shaping the environment, the Interpre-

tive Center uses fire to control underbrush on over 40 percent of the pine savanna. The fires bring an uncommon beauty to the woods as the charcoaled bark flakes off the pine trunks, revealing the ruddy, almost flesh tones of the new bark.

Fire also holds darker memories for the region—the class struggles of the South that fueled barn burnings and arson in Mississippi. Such associations and other cultural memories are not present at the Crosby Arboretum because the site is intended to be an optimistic landscape that looks to the future.

Fay Jones's architecture for Pinecote is an elaboration of the site and an expression of its ecology. The pavilion is constructed of pine lumber harvested near Picayune, is oriented to capture favorable breezes, and is sited on the north/south axis so that on the equinoxes, the sun sets directly on the end of the east-west pathway. The pavilion is a secular variation of Jones's series of cathedrals, which began with his famous Thorncrown Chapel in Eureka Springs, Arkansas. All the buildings in this

A delicate water primrose (*Ludwigea repens*) peeks out beneath a bridge designed by Fay Jones.

Lichens cover the trunks of
the red maples near the pond.

The Pavilion's thin wooden columns echo the trunks of the native pine trees.

The round nutlets of the buttonbush (*Cephalanthus occidentalis*) persist through the winter.

series are a transformation of the exterior masonry bracing of Gothic cathedrals into delicate wooden interior cross bracing, using two-by-fours. The Pinecote Pavilion is both larger and lower than Thorncrown Chapel—which is set in very hilly terrain—so as to spread itself over the flat landscape.

For every project, whether sacred or secular, Jones identifies a generating idea, usually a geometric motif. At Pinecote, Jones explains, "The whole building is ordered by a stepped-edge pattern that defines the outline of the floor and of the roof's outer edges. That pattern also allows the roof to spread out without being hard edged. The roof has a central skylight and plays out at the edges where the framing isn't covered so the pattern creates a gradual transition. I wanted to go from what is definitely out in the woods—not covered—to some-

thing that is definitely covered, and the open roof frame provides a transition, or a kind of middle landscape as I call it, where you're not quite inside or out."[13] Jones also roots the Pinecote Pavilion firmly in the region by attention to details of materials and construction. The compound columns are constructed with two-by-fours milled not far from the site and are thinly notched to link them visually to the segmented bark of the slash pines. The sharp angles of the bracing for the roof are roughly the same as those of the upper branches of the pines, and the brick floor of the pavilion almost matches the red clay of the Interpretive Center's paths. As the wood ages to a greenish-gray and the landscape grows larger around it, the pavilion will be appreciated as a poetically measured shelter, a constant against which the evanescent drama of nature can be apprehended.

The pond in which the pavilion is reflected is just as carefully controlled by a Fay Jones—designed dam that reiterates the stepped pattern of the pavilion. Near the pavilion Jones designed a masterful series of bridges, benches, and drinking fountains (more will be added to the rest of the site), which are also based on the pavilion's stepped pattern. This repetition insures that every piece of the site is part of the whole and serves, Jones hopes, as "a signal that stirs intelligent and eventful responses to the environment."[14] Pinecote rewards patience by faithfully rendering the region's small ups and downs, its damp and sunny patches, all of which are quietly transforming the landscape.

PROJECT : **THE CROSBY ARBORETUM: PINECOTE, THE NATIVE PLANT CENTER**

CLIENT : **THE CROSBY ARBORETUM FOUNDATION; ANNE S. BRADBURN, PRESIDENT; LYNN CROSBY GAMMILL, FORMER PRESIDENT.**

DATE OF COMPLETION : **1979—Present**

LOCATION : **PICAYUNE, MISSISSIPPI**

MASTER PLAN : **EDWARD BLAKE, JR., AND ANDROPOGON ASSOCIATES, LTD.**

ARCHITECT : **FAY JONES AND MAURICE JENNINGS ARCHITECTS**
PRINCIPAL-IN-CHARGE: **FAY JONES**

DIRECTOR : **EDWARD BLAKE, JR.**

SUPERINTENDENT : **CHRISTOPHER J. WELLS**

CONSULTANTS : **DR. SIDNEY T. McDANIEL, BOTANIST**

CURATOR OF COLLECTIONS : **ROBERT BRUSZEK**

The long bridge provides an ideal vantage point to observe the different ecosystems and patterns of natural succession in and around the pond.

FOUR

THE ESSENTIAL FORM

After World War II, there were designers and artists in every field who were determined to carry contemporary theoretical propositions to their inexorable conclusions. Historians encouraged these explorations by describing art as a series of progressive "isms," moving from impressionism to abstract expressionism and, by implication, to future "isms." Instead of teaching the reigning style in the manner of seventeenth-century French academies and salons, postwar universities, art schools, and art galleries urged students and young artists to seek new forms and theories.

One new theory—stylistic austerity in all artistic disciplines—led to what was loosely termed "minimal" or "reductivist" art. In the visual arts, minimalism was a reaction to the intemperate elaborations and proliferations of consumerism. Visual artists could comment on these perceived excesses by producing work that featured reductivist geometry and unelaborated, "honest" materials. Landscape designers endeavored to reduce landscape design to the equivalent of a prime number: something that was no longer divisible. But unlike studio artists, landscape designers also had to answer programmatic needs, such as seating or shade, and explain their design to the client. Though these concerns might have been considered unforgivable compromises to a minimalist sculptor, modern landscape designers found human meaning and significance in minimal forms, especially in their relationship to the larger environment.

Proponents of reductivism argue that as the world grows more complex and frenetic, only strong minimal forms are even objectively visible in the chaotic continuum of the modern landscape. The counterargument is that geometry had more meaning in the pre-industrial age, before perfect geometry was mass-produced and rendered common. But the fact is that the formal, archetypal qualities of a circle, a square, a single line, and other primary forms have endured throughout history and technological change. The challenge is to re-present the primary forms, not as empty symbolic gestures or recondite artistic theory, but as modern places for rituals and communal events. Reductivist landscape designers answer that challenge by re-establishing primary forms within the spatial continuum of daily life, so that functionalism, honest materialism, and myth are united in their iconic landscape designs.

PALEY
PARK

N E W   Y O R K   C I T Y
N E W   Y O R K

One of the greatest inspirations of modern landscape architecture was the "vest-pocket" park—a rational and welcome infusion of nature into the leftover interstices of the modern city. The term suggests the smallest possible opening in the city fabric, as well as the polish and sophistication it bestows upon its user. The most perfect of these, Paley Park in New York City, has become one of Manhattan's treasures, a masterpiece of urbanity and grace. Ironically, it was intended to be one of a hundred such parks, in a network so ubiquitous that each park would be as wonderfully ordinary as the cafes of Paris. Indeed, Paley Park first came into being not as a design for a specific client and a specific site, but as part of landscape architect Robert Zion's proposal—at once modest and monumental—that citizens build a vest-pocket park on *every* midtown block. Together, this matrix of small parks would create a countercurrent to the rush of urban activity, offering idylls and eddies in which to pause and gather strength before venturing back into the exhilarating rapids of the city streets. The idea was and is so simple and so obvious in its appeal to beauty and utility that the only criticism one can level at Paley Park is that there are *not* hundreds just like it.

Zion's initial problem was to persuade New Yorkers that a small alley or vacant lot could in fact become a park. From the opening of Olmsted's Central Park in the mid-nineteenth century through the turn-of-the-century City Beautiful movement to the urban renewal plans of the mid-twentieth century, city planners focused their attention on large parks, ceremonial civic plazas, avenues, and park-

The gate, which is not closed until 10:00 P.M. during the summer months, allows passersby to see into the park.

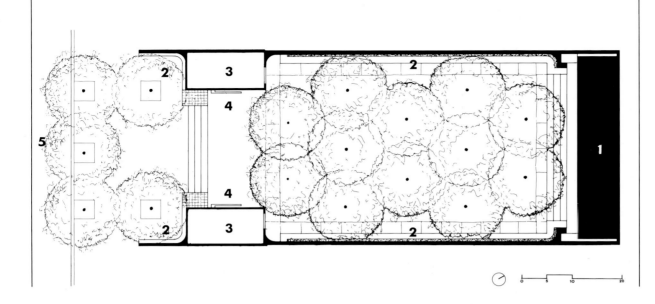

ways. Zion (1922–) scoffed at the accepted truism that a viable urban park needed a minimum of three acres to accommodate city crowds, and argued that New York would be better served by thousands of very small parks. And instead of trying to emulate European urban experiences—as the monumentally empty American plazas of the 1960s attempted to do—Zion sought to satisfy America's desire for a *simultaneous* embrace of city and country.

Zion and his partner Harold Breen prepared an exhibition of their work for the Architectural League in New York in 1963, and in it they included a speculative design proposal for a then-empty lot at 56th Street and Fifth Avenue. Every important feature eventually realized in Paley Park was illustrated in the exhibition design and Zion succinctly defined the concept as "a room, with walls, floors and ceiling."[1] Since it was a room, the park had movable chairs instead of standard park benches, but it was important to Zion that the park avoid resembling a Victorian sitting room with ornamental flowers, treillage, and small fountains or statuary. Zion stressed that the park would be straightforward so that hundreds like it could easily be built and maintained. Rugged trees planted on a regular grid would create a geometrical order in harmony with the city grid, and species with light foliage were preferred so as not to create dense shade in the already dark corridors of town. The water would be bold and simple—not a garden fountain or goldfish pond—and would provide what designers call "white noise," a neutral sound that overwhelms the urban clamor. The tree trunks would create a "bold and restful silhouette," and together with the cooling sound of the falling water, offer succor to frazzled urbanites. The walls of the room—formed by the exterior walls of the enclosing buildings—would be planted with vines to become "vertical lawns." Food kiosks would offer light refreshments and the floor's paving would have texture and interest, but be durable and easily maintained. Flowers would be confined to common planters—a plain box of impatiens would be preferred to more exotic or complicated floriferous displays. Finally, the room's fencing, if needed to close the park late at night, would be penetrable visually so pedestrians could easily see into the park.

Fortuitously, the Architectural League exhibition caught the eye of William S. Paley, head of CBS, who had been casting about for an appropriate memorial to his recently deceased father, Samuel. Coincidentally, Paley had bought a vacant site, formerly occupied by the Stork Club, and its location at 53rd Street and Fifth Avenue happened to be only three blocks from Zion's imaginary park. Paley's property was only slightly smaller than the exhibition design—today's Paley Park is 42 by 100

The four broad steps are a
threshold that raises the park
above the sidewalk and out of
the frantic pace of city life.

The chairs were designed by Harry Bertoia and the white marble tables by Eero Saarinen. They are movable, allowing users to arrange themselves as if they were in their own living rooms.

feet, compared to the exhibition's 50 by 100 feet. Zion and Breen didn't simply build the exhibition design, but made a series of refinements, all of which have contributed to the park's success. The number of honey locusts was reduced from twenty-four to twelve, and the trees were planted in a quincunx instead of the exhibition's regular grid. The quincunx relaxed the canopy of trees and allowed their silhouettes to be more apparent. Zion and Breen tried out fanciful kiosks before settling on a discreet, seven-and-a-half-foot-wide brick pavilion that frames the entrance and offers beverages and snacks. They also added four broad steps at the entrance—just high enough to make users feel they are lifted above the city crowds, yet low enough to give passersby a clear view of the water wall. Architectural panels were proposed for the side walls until Zion and Breen decided it was simpler, less expensive, and more honest to leave the rough brick walls of the adjoining buildings and let Boston ivy cover them. Kudzu vines were considered until former Southerners warned that the

vines might be too verdant for the small park.[2]

New York's first privately financed public park, Paley Park is memorable because it makes no effort to be so. The only hint of commemoration is a small plaque dedicating the park to Samuel Paley. There is no sculpture or any reference to the site's history—design strategies that became de rigueur for urban parks twenty years later. Zion understood that the significance of vest-pocket parks is that they offer refuge from the mental and sensory overload of working, shopping, or other urban activities. The space is more important than any image or subject; recuperative contact with natural elements is more important than any object within the park.

Paley Park's most striking feature is its "bold and simple" twenty-foot-high water wall, over which pour 1,800 gallons of water a minute. Users agree that the sound of the water is pleasant and soothing; they might be quite surprised to realize that the sound, when isolated from the visual qualities of the park, is anything but pleasurable. When sociologist William Whyte made an audio tape of the fountain and played it without identification, people winced and guessed it to be the roar of a subway or freeway.[3] But park users don't really "hear" the sound because it is continuous, while the street noise is erratic and staccato, and because they associate it with the visual beauty of the park. The water wall not only masks random traffic noise, but even drowns out voices at adjoining tables, enabling intimate conversation despite the crowded seating.

As utopian or naive as Zion's proposal for a park on every midtown block might now seem to the average New Yorker, the Architectural League exhibition actually reflected the pragmatism of Zion's academic background, which includes masters degrees from Harvard in both landscape architecture and business. Zion wrote that businesses should support vest-pocket parks because "a worker who returns refreshed is a more productive worker."[4] Zion also reasoned that the city itself should not pay for such parks, because their presence removes real estate from the tax rolls. Since the surrounding offices and shops benefit financially— "the weary shopper can rest and return refreshed

to shopping"—neighboring commercial enterprises should consider the low costs of maintaining a park a shrewd investment. And on a larger scale, Zion argued, the improved image of New York as a city of small parks would appeal to tourism, a "billion-dollar business." Vest-pocket parks were not to be volunteer-tended victory gardens or local garden-club displays; they would be built and maintained by hard-headed businesspeople whose companies would reap financial reward and public approbation.

Zion's exhibition notes echoed the ideas of Alphonse Alphand, author of *Les Promenades de Paris* (1869), a manual of the Paris park system. Seeking to bring nature into the city, Alphand incorporated a country amenity, the "promenade," into the dense fabric of Paris. As historian Antoine Grumbach observes: "One of the conditions for the creation of beauty in the city achieved by Alphand was that it could be named, measured, and tallied: any superfluous beauty was inconceivable in this age of materialism."[5] "Art is beauty realized by utility," wrote Alphand's superior, Baron Hauss-

The honey locust trunks form abstract compositions against the water wall.

mann. In a similar way, thanks in large measure to the tireless advocacy of William Whyte, New York codified its vest-pocket parks and small plazas in the 1975 Zoning Amendment. Developers could receive a square-footage bonus for their building by providing such amenities as "one linear foot of seating for each thirty square feet of open space."

But unlike Alphand's parks, which were created with an eye to the organic integrity of the city by designers who felt they were doing a public service, Paley Park's scattered progeny were designed and built to call attention to themselves instead of to the city as a whole. Some park-sponsoring clients have asked their designers for a park "like Paley— only more so."[6] But to try, as many New York vest-pocket parks have done, to augment Zion's prescription with architectural embellishment, horticultural displays, public art collections, or other over-programming is self-aggrandizement at the expense of the larger public realm. Also unfortunate are the parks that adopt some of Paley's features— most often the water wall—but neglect such vital details as the four broad entrance steps that make the park a *room*. The most poignant indication of the disjunction between the aspirations of New York's Zoning Amendment and its implementation are the signs in front of each Manhattan vest-pocket park baldly informing citizens that the space is a public park because it conforms to zoning regulations.

When Paley Park opened in 1968, it did inspire some business leaders to propose similar parks. Unfortunately, many of these dreams withered during the recessions of the 1970s or were paid only lip service in the boom market of the 1980s—the property on which Paley Park stands is worth far more today than when the park was built, and it was very expensive even then. As Ada Louise Huxtable commented when Paley announced his gift to the city: "The thought of this kind of use for prime land in New York makes real estate men blanch. . . . Obviously, only public action or private philanthropy can make the small-park dream possible."[7] But both Zion and Paley believed that when Paley Park opened, its obvious virtues would inspire emulation. Zion recalls being quite nervous

The soothing sound of the water, the delicate foliage of the honey locust trees, and the intimate groupings of tables and chairs offer welcome respite to weary New Yorkers. OPPOSITE

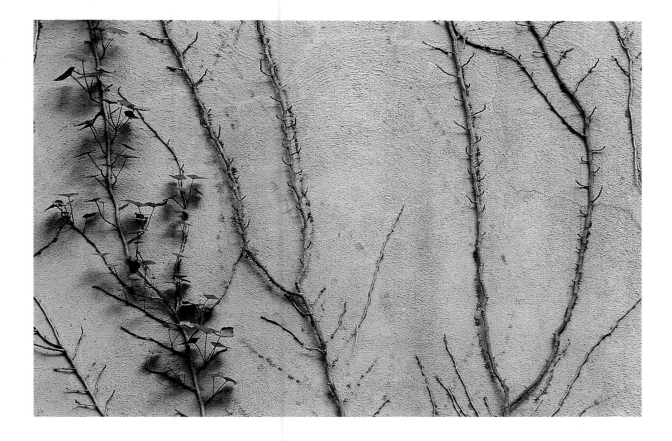

The calligraphy of Boston ivy inscribed on one of the walls enclosing the park.

at the water test shortly before the opening, since Paley himself was waiting impatiently.[8] Suddenly, with an enormous roar, the tumultuous cascade burst over the wall. Positioned between the rational city of commerce and architecture and the raw power of water, Zion and Paley watched as the water drowned out the noise of the city and imagined that vest-pocket parks like Paley would become, in Zion's words, "not amenities, but necessities of city life."[9]

PROJECT: **PALEY PARK**

CLIENT: **WILLIAM S. PALEY FOUNDATION**

DATE OF COMPLETION: **1967**

LOCATION: **NEW YORK, NEW YORK**

LANDSCAPE ARCHITECT: **ZION & BREEN ASSOCIATES, INC.**

GENERAL CONTRACTOR: **ROBERT JOHNSON, INC.**

PLUMBING CONTRACTOR: **E. KALISCH, INC.**

ELECTRICAL CONTRACTOR: **S. J. O'BRIEN COMPANIES**

GAS
WORKS
PARK

S E A T T L E
W A S H I N G T O N

Landscape architect Richard Haag's proposal to incorporate the hulking remains of a long-defunct Seattle gas-generating plant into a new city park was highly controversial in 1971, and it would be controversial today, too, but for different reasons. When the idea was proposed, the major controversy was whether or not the ruins of the generating plant should be incorporated into a city park. Today, questions of toxicity, safety, and other environmental concerns might well have made the planning effort too time-consuming and expensive. And though the environmental issues are still not settled to everyone's satisfaction, Gas Works Park is today one of the most heavily used and beloved parks in the Northwest.

Gas Works Park is a radically empirical design that employs visually powerful earth forms to order a public landscape. Because so much effort was expended by Haag and others to retain the plant structures, it is easy to overlook the fact that they were not "preserved" in any historical or curatorial sense of the word. Instead, the structures are celebrated and utilized for what they are—not for what they have been or for what they symbolize. Haag took a site that was filled with specific history and abstracted its formal qualities in one of the first attempts at adaptive re-use—a strategy that would later blossom at Faneuil Hall Market in Boston and other urban centers.

In 1906, on the north shore of Seattle's midcity Lake Union, the Seattle Gas Company built a large plant to extract gas from coal. Seen from a

Gas Works Park's Great Mound is one of the best places in Seattle to launch a kite.

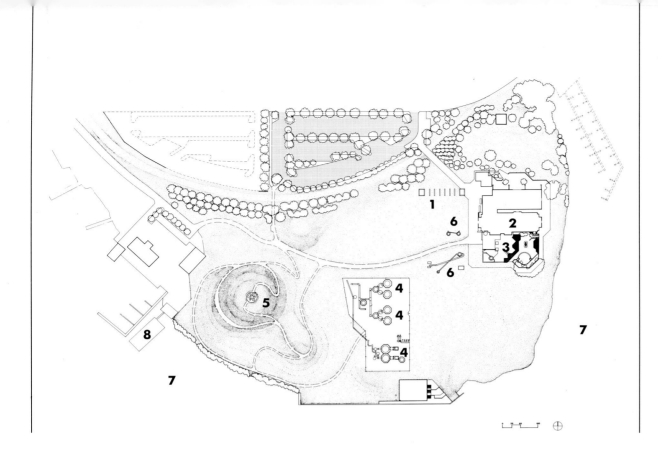

GAS WORKS PARK

1. VIADUCTS
2. PLAY BARN
3. OUTDOOR PLAYGROUND
4. GENERATING TOWERS
5. SUNDIAL ON TOP OF GREAT MOUND
6. OLD GAS PLANT EQUIPMENT
7. LAKE UNION
8. HARBOR PATROL—NOT PART OF PARK

distance, the shower of sparks looked beguiling, but for decades nearby residents complained bitterly about the air pollution. Still, the plant continued to operate until 1956, when the construction of a natural gas pipeline made the plant's extraction processes obsolete.

At the time, Seattle had no public park on Lake Union, which was ringed with a mix of industry and residential enclaves. So in 1962, the city purchased the gas plant's twenty-acre site and the gas company agreed to remove the plant machinery and structures from the property by the time of final payment in 1973. The new park was to be named after Myrtle Edwards, the councilwoman who had championed the cause of the new park.

Everyone assumed that the cleared site would be replanted with trees and lawns. Landscape architect Richard Haag (1923–   ) organized a student design competition for the park, and of 130 entries, not one proposed to save the plant structures. Nor, at that time, did it occur to Haag himself, he is now chagrined to admit.

By 1970, when Haag's firm was commissioned to prepare a master plan for the new park, the

structures were still standing in a miasma of oily wastes, because the gas company had suspended its demolition operations due to a drop in the price of scrap iron. Instead of working from topographic maps, Haag began to investigate the site first-hand, climbing the old towers and even camping out on the site. Gradually, he developed an intense emotional bond with the structures and began to have recurring dreams about them. In one particularly vivid dream, the gas works were the only thing left standing after a nuclear war, and people crawled out of the ruins to begin restoring the city.[1] Haag moved his offices into one of the plant's shops, encouraged visitors to explore the works, and organized a citizens' group to promote the idea of saving the industrial relics. Haag's advocacy had a strong countercultural appeal in the polarized climate of the time and his willingness to take on the establishment gained him both friends and enemies.

As he was marshaling support, Haag dwelled not on the plant's history, but on the forms of the structures themselves. In talks with community groups, students, design professionals, politicians, and any-

The old gas works was chosen as the site for a city park because it was the only substantial open space remaining on Seattle's Lake Union.

one else who would listen, Haag alternated slides of modern steel sculpture with slides of the gas plant, encouraging people to view the structures as abstract art—"unselfconscious assemblages" he called them, a label that denies the plant's very conscious assemblage, engineering, and former function. Although Haag's deep personal response to the towers did involve a connection to their history, his attitude as a designer was graphically illustrated in a series of sketch proposals by landscape architect Laurie Olin, then working in his office. All of Olin's drawings treat the plant purely as an *objet trouvé* or as a "good visual anchor for the park." Olin wrote: "Any good designer would jump at the chance to work out some of the motifs implied in the great iron and rivet vocabulary. . . . Remember the great lifts in the Tour Eiffel. . . . Will grown American men let down their hair enough to play in a huge sandbox—why not?—the hippies have shown the way for us all to learn to play in public. . . . The Plant becomes a honeycomb of various athletics and recreations (a sort of pinball machine with people in it)."[2] None of these visions refer to the history of the plant, because Haag and

Olin were responding directly to the phenomena of the structures and valued them more for what they might become than for how they might express the past.

While Haag had encouraged people to come forward with ideas for the park, he reserved the actual design of the park for himself, explaining, "There was no public participation in the *design*. Just because people had a lot of enthusiasm and love for those towers didn't mean they knew anything about designing a park. How can you expect a solution to come from somebody who's never really thought about space and how hard it is to create pure space in a park?"[3] Haag submitted his master plan in November 1971; it focused on the adaptive re-use of the plant structures as play barns, galleries, restaurants, cinemas, and almost everything else that might fit under a roof. The master plan also included marinas, a lake-front promenade, and a "Great Mound."

The plan was lengthily debated in letters to the editors, radio talk shows, and other public forums. The family of Mrs. Myrtle Edwards indignantly requested that—if built—Haag's proposed park not be named in her honor. Finally, in August of 1972, the city council unanimously approved the master plan. Due to the city's limited budget, the park was to be built in phases.

The difficulties of turning the site into the kind of lush arboretum that flourishes in Seattle's mild climate became apparent when tests revealed highly polluted ground conditions. Some areas were so toxic that one soil expert fainted when he descended into a test pit, and throughout the site, the subsurface contained a labyrinth of concrete foundations, old pipes, waste pits, and other industrial debris. During the construction of the park, an estimated eight miles of pipe and hundreds of truckloads of contaminated soil and debris were removed.

Ernie Ferrero, Chief Project Manager for the Seattle Department of Parks and Recreation, remembers that when the park was built the conventional wisdom was to "cap it with some clay and topsoil and hope things would grow. The environmental impact statement dealt more with traffic noise than with toxicity. We knew there was benzene

and even cyanide, but all we knew was that they weren't compatible with water, plants, or human beings. Nobody had studied long-term health hazards."[4] Haag's strategies for soil-detoxification were ahead of current engineering practice and relied heavily on the advice of soil expert Richard Brooks, who encouraged him to try organic filtering.[5] Oil-eating enzymes, lawn clippings, sewage sludge, and other organic materials were tilled into the soil. The process was repeated several times and some of the worst soil was used as the base of the Great Mound. The entire site was then capped with fill dirt from unrelated nearby construction. Composted sludge was also used to augment the fill dirt and, in its first summer, sprouted a field of tomatoes and melons. But the subsoil remained

toxic and there have been problems with continued leaching into Lake Union. However, the city of Seattle now realizes that the entire lake needs much stricter environmental controls, and water pollution from Gas Works is viewed as part of a much larger problem.

In the first phase of the park's construction, Haag turned the boiler house, the lowest structure, into a picnic shelter. The exhaust house became a children's play barn by transforming some of the old equipment into a brightly painted jungle gym. Haag observes that this freewheeling playground, which gives children the chance to turn the old machinery into their own fantasies and athletic challenges, would not pass the latest safety standards. As architecture historian Sally Woodbridge

The park is used for everything from kite-flying to political demonstrations.

The top of the former exhaust house, which has been brightly painted and converted into a children's play barn. LEFT

Appendages were stripped from the old gas plant equipment to prevent youths from climbing the pipes. The large towers in the background have been fenced off. BELOW

recently lamented, current playgrounds are sterile compared to Gas Works's play barn: "These are the realities of the litigious world we live in, where liability for injuries mandates a risk-free area for play. The limitations of this situation beset designers who struggle to create play environments that encourage the young to explore, to experiment and to test their limits so that, as adults, they can contribute creatively to life on this planet."[6] The park opened to the public in September 1975, and construction of the first phase continued through 1978, creating pathways down to the water's edge and landscaping the parking lot and the old railroad bed.

The master plan called for adaptive re-use of the towers as well, and included a vertical circulation system that would lead to a camera obscura chamber, stations for viewing the park and Lake Union, exercise facilities, and rooms for other activities. There was not enough money in the initial phase to adapt the main cooling towers, but visually they were the most prominent structures—Haag called the largest one, nearest the lake, the "Great Mother." He stripped off most of the towers'

appendages, but after several accidents in which reckless young boys were hurt trying to climb them, the towers were fenced off with chain link and barbed wire. Constructed of half-inch-thick steel, the towers are in no immediate danger of collapse, but their incomplete development obscures some of the clarity of the original master plan.

Much of the grading throughout the park looks crude, partly because the different types of soil did not settle evenly. But the strength of the park's design comes from its use of elemental landscape forms that are in scale with the gas plant structures. Since the relatively open site plan encourages raucous urban activities instead of passive relaxation or contemplation, its forms had to be as tough as the steel towers so the park could take the hard wear of festivals and other temporary events.

The landscape was structured to facilitate both circulation and observation. To the north Haag planted trees along the old rail spur to create a threshold for visitors arriving from the parking lot, which fronts noisy Northlake Way. A wide swale leads visitors from the parking lot to the waterfront between the Great Mound and the hulking cooling

An elaborate sundial by artists Chuck Greening and Kim Lazare tops the Great Mound.

towers. The Mound offers a panoramic view of the park and Lake Union, while the towers, at virtually the same height, will someday offer carefully framed views. The concrete viaducts from the plant's former coal ramps visually contain the park and direct visitors toward the play barn.

One of Haag's last additions to the park was a sundial on top of the Great Mound, created by artists Chuck Greening and Kim Lazare. A person stands in the center of it, acting as the gnomon, or indicator, and reads the time by his or her own shadow. The challenge of deciphering the time (which involves adding or subtracting minutes and hours depending on the season), as well as the sundial's complicated inscriptions and astrological signs, add to the visitors' enjoyment. The sundial might have been an opportunity to connect the users of the park with its history, but instead, the device literally points to the present moment. Standing on the Great Mound, visitors cast a shadow that marks the current time, while the dark shadows of yesterday's towers quietly recede.

During the 1980s, when environmental standards became much stricter, the EPA conducted numerous studies of the park that delayed further development and even closed the grounds for six months in 1984—the park needed some additional fill and paving. When it reopened, it did so with one of the most unusual signs ever posted in such a heavily used park:

NOTICE

THIS PARK AND ADJACENT LAKE CONTAIN HAZARDOUS SUBSTANCES

Gas Works Park is the site of a former gasification plant, which deposited materials now identified as hazardous substances on the site. In order to prevent human contact with contaminants,

Detail of the sundial.

some park areas have been closed temporarily for cleaning and repair and other areas have been covered with clean fill. In order to avoid contact with contaminants, park users should follow these rules:

1. KEEP OUT OF THE CLOSED AREAS
2. EXERCISE CAUTION WHEN PICNICKING
   Avoid direct contact with dirt (eating contaminated dirt over a long period is the only significant health risk)
3. DO NOT PLACE FOREIGN OBJECTS IN YOUR MOUTH
4. DO NOT SWIM
5. DO NOT WADE
6. DO NOT FISH

Additional tests will continue to determine the nature of any environmental risks at the park.

Haag's master plan provided a framework for many different activities, and in the past decade Gas Works Park has served equally well for kite-flying contests, chili cook-offs, the starting gate and finish line of running marathons, family reunions, auto shows, concerts, political demonstrations, and Fourth of July fireworks extravaganzas—the latter perhaps reminding the city's oldest residents of the old gas plant's fiery displays.

In 1968, several years before Haag had determined to save the plant, Kenneth Read, then Chairman of the University of Washington's Anthropology Department, published a poetic appeal for the preservation of the gas works' ruins:

They have a peculiar, yearning urgency . . . Hieronymus Bosch alive and well in Seattle . . . a lurid vision of apocalypse . . . [belonging] to a time when Orwellian visions of depersonalized efficiency were still remote. . . . In its own way it is a lesson comparable to Marmes Man [an archeological excavation in western Washington that yielded thousands of prehistoric tools]. Nothing quite like it has been created since. History sits on this little wasteland, not only the parochial history of a given city but also a fragment of the chronicle of world culture. It is certainly as valua-

ble a document as anything preserved in the Museum of History and Industry.[7]

None of these historical memories and visions found their way into Gas Works Park. Instead of a "lurid vision of apocalypse," one finds the unintentionally humorous EPA sign. Replacing Read's Orwellian vision is a children's play barn. As for industrial archeology, so much of the mechanical apparatus has been removed that it is now impossible to mentally reconstruct any of the plant's operations.

But if the past is not remembered, neither is it rewritten, and it would be unfair to see the park as a reactionary design intended to lull or muffle unpleasant history. It was difficult enough to persuade the city to save any part of the gas plant at all, and as the park ages, the dramatic steel dinosaurs may yet take on new life. Inspired by the logic of dreams, Gas Works Park is structured on the empirical reality of its materials and space.

PROJECT: **GAS WORKS PARK**

CLIENT: **SEATTLE DEPARTMENT OF PARKS AND RECREATION**

DATE OF COMPLETION: **1975 (OPENED TO THE PUBLIC)**

LOCATION: **SEATTLE, WASHINGTON**

LANDSCAPE ARCHITECT: **RICHARD HAAG ASSOCIATES, INC.**

ARTISTS: **CHARLES GREENING, KIM LAZARE**

ARCHITECTS: **MICHAEL G. AINSLEY; OLSEN/WALKER & ASSOCIATES**

STRUCTURAL ENGINEERS: **ARNOLD, ARNOLD & ASSOCIATES**

MECHANICAL ENGINEERS: **MISKIMEN/ASSOCIATES**

ELECTRICAL ENGINEERS: **BEVERLY A. TRAVIS & ASSOCIATES**

CONTRACTORS: **BORDNER CONSTRUCTION COMPANY; DAVISCOURT CONSTRUCTION COMPANY; GEORGE ADAMS**

The skyline of Seattle from the swale between the old gas towers to the left and the Great Mound to the right.

THE TANNER FOUNTAIN

C A M B R I D G E
M A S S A C H U S E T T S

When the low cloud of fine mist is not pulsing in the center of the Tanner Fountain, the passerby might not realize that the circular field of small boulders is, in fact, a fountain. Its placement amid asphalt paths and a grass lawn looks arbitrary, yet the stones themselves are so obviously secure and confident within their prescribed circle that the surrounding environment is hardly noticeable. Whether the water is on or off, the Tanner Fountain controls the ground the way a commanding orator "holds the floor" even without a microphone or podium.

The stones—each approximately four by two by two feet—are typical New England granite boulders, like those often found in the fan-shaped trails of successive glacial movements. Believed by early explorers to be evidence of the receding water line of the Great Flood, these glacial formations left boulders of all shapes and sizes obdurately entrenched, much to the frustration of early New England farmers trying to clear their fields. The Tanner Fountain boulders are also partially buried and display the same sense of permanence. Hard, heavy, and bulky, the corners knocked off but not polished, with a surface of dull mottled colors flecked with mica and other minerals, they are noble in their simplicity.

A number of contemporary artists have used boulders in totemic or ritualistic formations to evoke the mystery of prehistoric stone monuments such as Stonehenge and Karnak. Some art critics believe these sculptures and environmental art pieces have great significance for modern culture. A passionate

View across the fountain toward Memorial Hall. The water obscures the center of the circle of stones, yet seems to draw the stones toward the center.

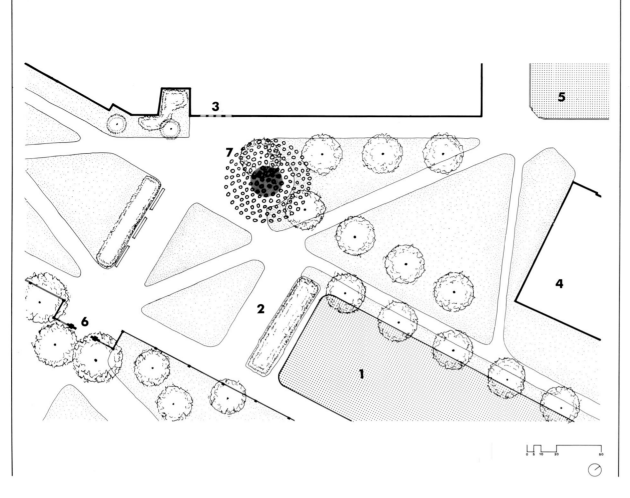

advocate of these artists is historian Lucy Lippard, who wrote, "Stones, still symbols of permanence, add new meanings to the old in the midst of our cultural disjunctions."[1] The Tanner Fountain also projects a sense of primary mystery, but the design's significance and authenticity do not depend on the appropriation of either prehistoric tribal architecture or contemporary art. Designed by the SWA Group as a practical solution to the problems of its particular site, the fountain is fundamentally invested in its own time and space. By refusing to contravene the fountain's social functions and formal geometry with overt symbolism or metaphor, the designer created Harvard University's first successful modern landscape design.

Harvard has seldom given the same deference or opportunities to landscape designers as it has to architects. Nearby Quincy Street is a veritable architectural zoo, exhibiting highly individualistic and assertive university buildings by Le Corbusier, H. H. Richardson, James Sterling, and John Andrews. But though the elms in historic Harvard Yard receive unceasing devotion, most of Harvard's large campus landscape is pleasant but banal. "Harvard has a kind of hair-shirt attitude towards the campus grounds. Aesthetics are considered a luxury," lamented Laurie Olin, former chairman of Harvard's Graduate Landscape Architecture Department.[2] Harvard's modern fountains have fared especially badly; because of the harsh climate and undependable maintenance, many have broken down and been filled in with flowers.

In 1979 Grace and Robert Tanner, who had previously sponsored fountains for Stanford University and Brigham Young University, donated money for a Harvard fountain of unspecified design and location, wisely setting aside a third of the relatively modest $400,000 bequest as a maintenance trust fund. The Tanners did not wish to be consulted about the fountain's design, but reserved the right to remain anonymous if they did not like the final result. Harvard commissioned the SWA Group to select an appropriate site.

In 1967 the university created a pedestrian

overpass to connect venerable Harvard Yard with the North Campus and Memorial Hall (built in 1870). Then, in 1973, Harvard's Science Center, a sprawling complex designed by José Luis Sert, was built on the north side of the overpass. The site of the heavily trafficked overpass contained some handsome trees but was otherwise an amorphous landscape with wide asphalt paths. The SWA Group chose to site the fountain on the overpass. Unfortunately, the budget did not allow them to redesign the entire overpass in order to create a more unified landscape for the fountain. So Peter Walker, consulting principal with the SWA Group and lead designer for the fountain, decided to use minimal means to make the fountain memorable, yet unobtrusive enough not to hamper future landscape improvements.

The water illuminates the mineral deposits imbedded in the surface of the boulders.

At the time the Tanner Fountain was being designed, Peter Walker had started a small experimental firm with some of his students from Harvard University, and sought commissions that offered unique formal design opportunities as a means of escaping the corporate complacency and the pleasant but unchallenging designs that too often marked the work of large landscape architecture firms.

Walker was intensely interested in the work of 1960s minimal artists such as Donald Judd, Dan Flavin, Carl Andre, and Walter de Maria. He even curated a New York gallery exhibition to champion the reductive aesthetic, which, he argued, "is usually the most refined expression of any age, not just the modern era, though modernism has focused on proportion and scale instead of decoration or detail."[3] Working with students and young design-

Historic Harvard Yard seems
to rise out of the fountain's
mist.

ers, Walker investigated ways in which landscape design could capture the uncompromising authority of the best minimal sculptures. When he revisited the work of André Le Nôtre (1613–1700), the designer of Versailles, Walker discovered that minimalism in landscape design could become the foundation of a new way of seeing the world. The association of Le Nôtre's opulent Baroque gardens with Carl Andre's *11 Blocks and Stones* (144 two-foot-square blocks of wood arranged in a grid on a gallery floor) surprised even Walker, but he realized that Le Nôtre had been able to control huge spaces with the same compositional strategies that minimalist artists would identify as flatness, pattern, seriality, dimensional extension, and repetition. Walker recalls: "When I went back to France and really studied those gardens, I began to see a strong connection between the way minimalist artists controlled gallery space and the way Le Nôtre controlled vast spaces with an equally limited vocabulary of forms. I wanted to find a way to use the lessons of minimalist spatial control to solve social and functional problems, and at the same time to go beyond function, beauty, and natural processes."[4]

"Seriality"—the repetitive use of an element or of intervals between elements to deny the individuality of the element in favor of the overall pattern—was one of the minimalist strategies Walker found particularly effective in the landscape. In his previous work, Walker had used stores in the manner of Japanese gardens, treasuring each one's singularity. At the Tanner Fountain, however, the boulders are like students whose individual characters exist within the embrace of a common discipline. The main criteria for selecting the boulders were that they be uniform in appearance and smooth on top for comfortable seating. The Tanner Fountain's seriality defines it as a circle separate from everything else. Even though the grass lawn was altered to accommodate the fountain jets, the stones may appear to have been set into the existing landscape.[5]

The circle gathers the space around it and draws one toward it. Walker investigated different circular patterns, such as radiating lines or a progression of different circles, before he settled on a field pattern that emphasized the circle itself, instead of any internal pattern. This pattern achieves what Walker calls a "minimalist garden without walls"—occupiable landscape designs that are not enclosed by walls and are not extensions of buildings, yet have a visual identity distinct from the surrounding landscape.[6]

The circular field of stones is reiterated at its center with a tantalizing cloud of fine water spray that shimmers above the middle stones. The small-caliber nozzles and the drains are below the level of the asphalt, so there is no conventional fountain basin. Artist Joan Brigham worked with the SWA Group to make the Tanner Fountain an "all-weather" phenomenon—in the winter, a cloud of steam drifts into the brisk New England air. The steam is vented from the Science Center heating ducts, which happen to pass directly underneath the fountain, but because of budget considerations, only 32 of the fountain's 102 nozzles emit steam. The vapor is visible only with the proper conjunction of light, temperature, and humidity, but on occasion its display, especially at night, can be quite magical. Fountain consultant Dick Chaix, who was disappointed with the steam effect, was further dismayed when technical problems were solved by enlarging the water jets—the summer mist now floats about a foot higher than originally designed. The larger spray is less mysterious, and on windy days the water can discourage people from sitting on the perimeter stones.

Walker's choice of New England stones for the fountain is an evocative regional response, but it is the archetypal, trans-cultural resonance of the circular field of boulders that has made the Tanner Fountain one of the icons of modern landscape design. The very universality of the circle and the materials used, however, makes it easy to mistake the Tanner Fountain for the work of contemporary British sculptor Richard Long, who brings stone, wood, or other natural materials from a particular location into a gallery or museum, where the material is arranged in totemic circles and other basic geometrical forms and connected by Long's photographs and documentation to the remote

landscapes of the material's origin. Another artistic influence on the Tanner Fountain is Carl Andre's *Stone Field Sculpture,* which occupies a triangular site in downtown Hartford, Connecticut. Andre's piece consists of 36 large boulders, some of them six feet high, arranged in eight rows with the interval between rows increasing as the size of the boulders in each row decreases.[7]

Some critics have questioned the artistic integrity of Walker's appropriation of form, but issues of signature style—which in today's art market is often the artist's most salable commodity—are not as relevant to site-specific works. In public landscape design, is the extension and *transformation* (there are many important differences between Long's work and Walker's design)[8] of the work of a contemporary artist any different from the use of historical precedents such as Haag's use of the canal at Courances (see page 58)? There is also the issue of integrity and intention. Walker's interest in the work of Long or Andre does not come from a need for stylistic appropriation, but from his ambition to extend the frontiers and artistic boundaries of landscape architecture beyond what he viewed as an over-emphasis on environmental concerns and social facilitation. While the Tanner Fountain owes an obvious debt to Long, Andre, and other artists, the significance and conceptual foundations of their art are quite different from those of landscape architecture. Walker maintains the critical distinction that "design *must* function while art *may* function."[9] Many of the formal qualities of the Tanner Fountain, such as the smooth tops and the height and spacing of the boulders, are explicitly designed to provide comfortable seating. In contrast, Long's circles are unoccupiable, and *Stone Field Sculpture* makes no concession to circulation; in fact, what landscape architects call a "desire line"—a worn path created by pedestrians who follow the shortest line between two points—cuts across the site, marring the purity of Andre's minimalist composition.

But Walker is clearly after more than utility, and the Tanner Fountain's materials possess meta-

With sunlight streaking through the mist, the boulders have a primordial grandeur.

phorical power. Historically, circles have been used as artistic representations of the cosmos or the heavens. In its university setting, the Tanner circle seems to float, both literally and symbolically, as if freed from the burdens of earthly labor. The boulders imply a sense of geological time, a poignant contrast to the transitory passages of student life.

But, while metaphorical speculation is pleasurable and, on the campus of Harvard University, inevitable, the most significant art of the Tanner Fountain is found in the straightforward facts of its materials and form. It is designed to embody as purely as possible something of its site and its region. Ralph Waldo Emerson—Harvard, class of 1821—might have been describing the Tanner Fountain when he wrote: "I ask not for Greek art. I embrace the common, I explore and sit at the feet of the familiar, below. Give me insight into today, and you may have the antique and future worlds."[10]

Peter Walker has called landscape design "a gift, a gift of understanding, a gift of delight, a gift of pleasure." When the Tanners saw Walker's gift, they did not hesitate to allow a donor's plaque to be tucked discreetly into the stone circle. They felt sure that the Tanner Fountain would prove as enduring as the boulders in New England's fields.

PROJECT: **TANNER FOUNTAIN**

CLIENT: **HARVARD UNIVERSITY**

DATE OF COMPLETION: **1985**

LOCATION: **HARVARD UNIVERSITY, CAMBRIDGE, MASSACHUSETTS**

LANDSCAPE ARCHITECT: **THE SWA GROUP WITH PETER WALKER**

PROJECT TEAM: **DUNCAN ALFORD, IAN KING, LISA ROTH**

CONTRACTOR: **MARTY JOYCE, BOND BROTHERS, INC.**

FOUNTAIN CONSULTANTS: **JOAN BRIGHAM**
CMS COLLABORATIVE
PARTNER-IN-CHARGE: **RICHARD CHAIX**

VIETNAM VETERANS MEMORIAL

WASHINGTON, D.C.

The Vietnam Veterans Memorial, completed in 1982, has directly affected more Americans than any other landscape design since World War II. The widely publicized story of the Memorial—the design competition, the subsequent battle for and against acceptance of the winning design, the controversial proposals for additions to it—and its role in transforming the emotional landscape of the Vietnam generation are issues so vital that it might seem secondary to discuss the Memorial's formal qualities. Yet for subsequent generations, the experience of the Vietnam Veterans Memorial will not be drawn from an immediate, personal connection with comrades, relatives, or the zeitgeist of the war years, but from the transitive relationships between designer Maya Lin's idea and the construction and maintenance of the Memorial. Formal issues that now appear to be marginal concerns are likely to become much more central in time.

It is important to understand that it is not only the *wall*, but the complete landscape design that is the Vietnam Veterans Memorial. Maya Lin (1960–   )[1] explains that the Memorial design was "a process applied to the earth . . . a process of cutting open the earth and polishing the exposed surface. The wall shouldn't have any mass. . . . it should just be a transparent plane. The mass is the earth itself. The polished surface gives the illusion of looking into the earth. An illusion, yet very real."[2]

Lin has been criticized for using a thin granite veneer instead of solid panels, which would have made the wall as substantial as the Wailing Wall

Early morning view of the Washington Monument from the Vietnam Veterans Memorial.

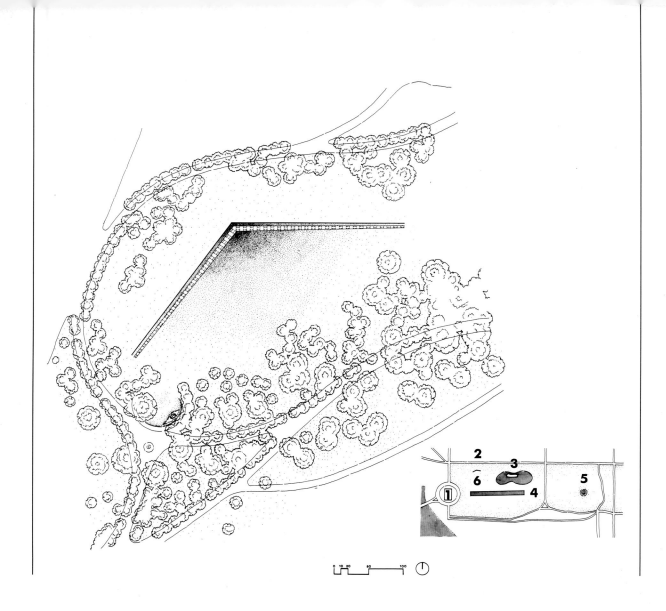

VIETNAM VETERANS MEMORIAL

1. LINCOLN MEMORIAL
2. CONSTITUTION AVENUE
3. CONSTITUTION GARDENS
4. REFLECTING POOL
5. WASHINGTON MONUMENT
6. THE WALL

in Jerusalem. However, solid panels would make the wall an object, whereas Lin's intention was to use the polished veneer to dematerialize the "wall-ness" of the granite. The polished granite panels inscribed with the names of the dead are as nondimensional and non-object as possible. From above and behind, the wall is hardly visible—one is aware only that the earth has been exposed.

A wall is a barrier, while the polished granite is a boundary. Philosopher Martin Heidegger suggested that a boundary "is not that at which something stops, but, as the Greeks recognized . . . that from which something begins its presencing."[3] At the Memorial, the boundary is the place from which the dead begin their presencing. Its southern exposure allows the sun to highlight the

inscribed names and to warm the backs of the living. A black light appears to emanate from the other side of the granite, brooding and insistent. It is not the names alone that turn the atmosphere funereal, but also the visceral intensity with which the living confront the profound depth of the other side. It is also a memorial for the living, who are literally reflected in the names of the dead, which are listed in the order in which they were killed, beginning with 1959 on the east side of the V-shaped wall's vertex and continuing until that side of the wall dies into the ground, then resuming at the end of the west side of the wall and continuing back to the vertex, so that the vertex is the divider between 1975 and 1959.[4] This chronological approach makes each name palpably present, placing it at its own moment in time, instead of linking it to the entire sixteen-year war.

It was Lin's original intention to have visitors approach the Memorial directly by walking down the sloping grass plane so that the names seem to rise *en masse*. The 125-degree angle of the V-shaped wall would then be experienced not as a midway point but as an epiphany. Approaching the wall in this way would have had particular significance for veterans, because, as so many of them know, when enemy lines are breached, the angle created by the attacking troops is where the greatest number of casualties is sustained. It is thus fitting that it is at the vertex of this angled wall that the chronology of names begins and ends: the first American casualty of the war on the right side and the last on the left. As Lin explained: "Thus the war's beginning and end meet: the war is 'complete,' coming full circle . . . and contained within the earth itself."[5]

Connection has been the central struggle in the realization of Lin's design. The connection of the granite panels to the earth is elegantly detailed along the top, but the connections between the grass slope, the path, and the panels have never been satisfactorily resolved, because of the difficulties of *techné*, which the Greeks defined as the art and craft of making an idea visible within the existing landscape. The difficulties of making Lin's conceptual design visible within the specific conditions of its site have left the Memorial fragmented by ad hoc decisions and aesthetically insensitive concessions to the exigencies of accommodating 5,000,000 visitors annually.

The Mall in Washington, D.C., is built on top of a swamp, and the Naval buildings that stood on the site of the Vietnam Veterans Memorial from World War I until the late 1950s compacted the soil, making the *techné* of building what Lin described as a "rift in the earth" formidable—walls simply do not emerge or recede gently into compacted soils with a high water table. What Lin envisioned as a "gentle slope" toward the vertex of the wall turned out to be too steep, given the soil conditions, to prevent visitors from churning the grass into mud. Eventually the Park Service cordoned off the slope, enforcing a descent and departure parallel to the wall. This creates a sequence that runs directly counter to Lin's idea of approaching the wall at the vertex, where the beginning and end of the war meet. Following the Park Service route, one would expect the chronology of names to begin at one end, build to the greatest concentration in the middle, and taper off at the other end—a time line mirroring the military history of the Vietnam War. If this were so, the viewer would either start at the beginning of the war or at the very last name and trace the war back to its origin. As it stands today, the failure of the designer's *techné* weakens the full experience of her idea.

Even before the competition, Lin realized that

the ideal of having grass grow right up to the base of the Memorial was impractical, so she designed a six-foot wide path parallel to the wall. She envisioned using crushed stone, which would be of the earth, in lieu of a hard paving material, which would rest on the earth. Crushed marl is used for the main paths on the Mall and has held up very well, but those paths are relatively level. Even though the length of the wall was extended ninety-three feet to accommodate handicap access, the slope of the Memorial path was still four percent—far too steep to hold crushed stone, especially in the compacted soils—so the path was constructed of polished gray granite and gradually tapered at

each end. A honed granite base stone was added as a mowing strip; it was visually unobtrusive and allowed mementos to be propped up against the wall. Less successful was the Park Service's extensions of the path at each end to link it up with the directories of names and with the paths leading to other parts of the Mall. These extensions have weakened the integral connection between the polished granite wall and the path.

Eventually, the crowds of visitors proved too much for the four-foot strip of grass between the path and the wall. The project architects, Cooper-Lecky, bordered the smooth granite pavers on each side with rough granite sets, and added ground

The panels reach a height of ten feet and stepladders are provided for those who want to make rubbings of the names near the top.

The mementos left along the wall are stored in a voluminous archive by the Park Service. OPPOSITE

lights for evening visitors. This solution is too complex; the melange of different materials distracts from the sublimity of the wall.

The strongest criticism of Lin's original plan came from those who wanted a more conventional memorial. The controversy was resolved, temporarily at least,[6] with the 1985 addition of Frederick Hart's bronze sculpture of three infantrymen, located at the top of the hill. The soldiers and the nearby American flag do not significantly affect the experience of the Memorial, however, because Hart's sculpture is a very different memorial conceptually, and its distance from Lin's wall might lead a viewer who does not possess an intimate knowledge of America's ambivalence toward the Vietnam War to assume that they are two separate memorials, perhaps even commemorating two separate events.[7]

Lin was more disturbed about the gradual additions to the path than about Hart's sculpture, especially since she was not consulted on the design decisions. She recently voiced her frustrations with the difficulty of trying to resolve problems of *techné* through the formidable Washington bureaucracy: "I don't mind the statues [Frederick Hart's infantrymen] as much as the path. I hate when things happen for no good reason or with no passion on anyone's part. I don't think anyone really wanted that path. It just happened and that's inexcusable."[8] In any reductive or essential design, the

Lin's original intention was for visitors to approach the V-shaped wall by walking down this grass slope toward the vertex.

Fragile flowers and American flags are particularly poignant against the polished black granite.

details become vitally important. Architect Louis Kahn was once exasperated by an associate who chided him about spending too much time on the plumbing details: "I don't love plumbing details—I hate them thoroughly! But if I just hated them and didn't pay attention to them, they would invade my building and destroy it."[9]

But for all those who have been touched by the Vietnam War and its times, any problems of *techné* and visitor accommodation dissolve in the face of the fifty-seven thousand names. Much of the credit for the success of the Vietnam Veterans Memorial is due to Jan Scruggs, President of the Vietnam Veterans Memorial Fund, which ran the competition. He proposed the competition requirement that the names of all 57,692 casualties be inscribed on the memorial. This requirement meant that any memorial design had to entail some kind of wall or field of large slabs or blocks. The other major requirement was the designated site—somewhere between the Lincoln Memorial and the Washington Monument. The fact that Lin's design projects toward the two memorials can be viewed merely as a convenient orientation. After all, what do Lincoln or Washington have to do with the Vietnam War? But many tourists consider all the memorials and monuments of Washington, D.C., a collective symbol of America. Those visitors descend to the vertex—which is the beginning and end of the war—then, as they ascend, they confront the monuments and, by symbolic extension, the political institutions that sent the soldiers to war.

Lin responded to the competition requirements by conceiving of a monument for both the living and the dead, inspired in part by Sir Edwin Lutyens's 1927–30 Memorial to the Missing of Somme at Thiepval, France, and the Mémorial de la Déportation in Paris, designed by G. H. Pingusson in 1962.[10] While there may be formal similarities between the Vietnam Veterans Memorial and minimalist art, Lin's reduction of symbolic and decorative elements should not be directly tied to the minimalists' investigations of industrial fabrication and mass production. The discourse of minimalism, along with that of the contemporaneous earth art

movement, addresses the perceptual and institutional definitions of art, while Lin's design, like those of Lutyens and Pingusson, is concerned with public commemoration.

The Lutyens memorial is a monumental arch at the entrance to a cemetery devoted to the dead of a single campaign—the Somme offensive—in World War I. The names of 73,357 French and British soldiers (15,000 more than on the Vietnam Memorial) are inscribed on the base of the arch. Standing there, the viewer is confronted with the immediacy of the individual names against the collective serenity of the hillside of crosses beyond.

The Mémorial de la Déportation, which remembers the 200,000 French Jews who died during the Nazi Holocaust, does not record individual names but is more stark and reductive than Lutyens's design. Set beneath l'Île de France Square in the shadow of Notre Dame, its emotional center is a long tunnel containing 200,000 dimly glowing quartz pebbles. Its entranceway is barred, so the tunnel itself becomes a metaphor for a gaping scream, evoking the haunting realization that one can never know the final resting place of these dead.

The Mémorial de la Déportation contains other iconography and specific reliquaries, including niches containing earth from concentration camps. But in Maya Lin's design, no iconography explicitly links the Vietnam Veterans Memorial with the Vietnam War. The meaning of the Memorial is certainly deepened by knowledge of the conflict and its times, but the more profound, archetypal meaning is accessible to all. "Death," wrote Lin, "is a personal and private matter."[11] The Vietnam Veterans Memorial is poised at the moment of passage from the world of light to the darkness beyond, giving visitors the opportunity for reflection on their own passage through life.

Lin has "composed the place," as St. Ignatius instructed in his *Spiritual Exercises,* by "focusing the mind and thought . . . within the bounds and limits of the subject."[12] Phenomenologically, the Vietnam Veterans Memorial composes a connection between earth and sky, enclosing the visitor in a vast net of correspondences and in the earth itself.

The chronology of names of the dead starts with 1959 to the right of the wall's vertex and finishes with 1974 to the left of the vertex. This central spot thus marks the beginning and end of the Vietnam War.

PROJECT: **VIETNAM VETERANS MEMORIAL**

CLIENT: **VIETNAM VETERANS MEMORIAL FUND**

DATE OF COMPLETION: **1982**

LOCATION: **WASHINGTON, D.C.**

OWNER: **NATIONAL PARK SERVICE**

DESIGNER: **MAYA YING LIN**

ARCHITECT OF RECORD: **COOPER-LECKY PARTNERSHIP**
DESIGN PARTNER: **W. KENT COOPER**

LANDSCAPE ARCHITECTS: **HENRY ARNOLD ASSOCIATES AND EDAW, INC.**

STRUCTURAL ENGINEER: **JAMES MADISON CUTTS**

CIVIL ENGINEER: **BERNARD F. LOCRAFT**

CONTRACTOR: **GILBANE BUILDING COMPANY**

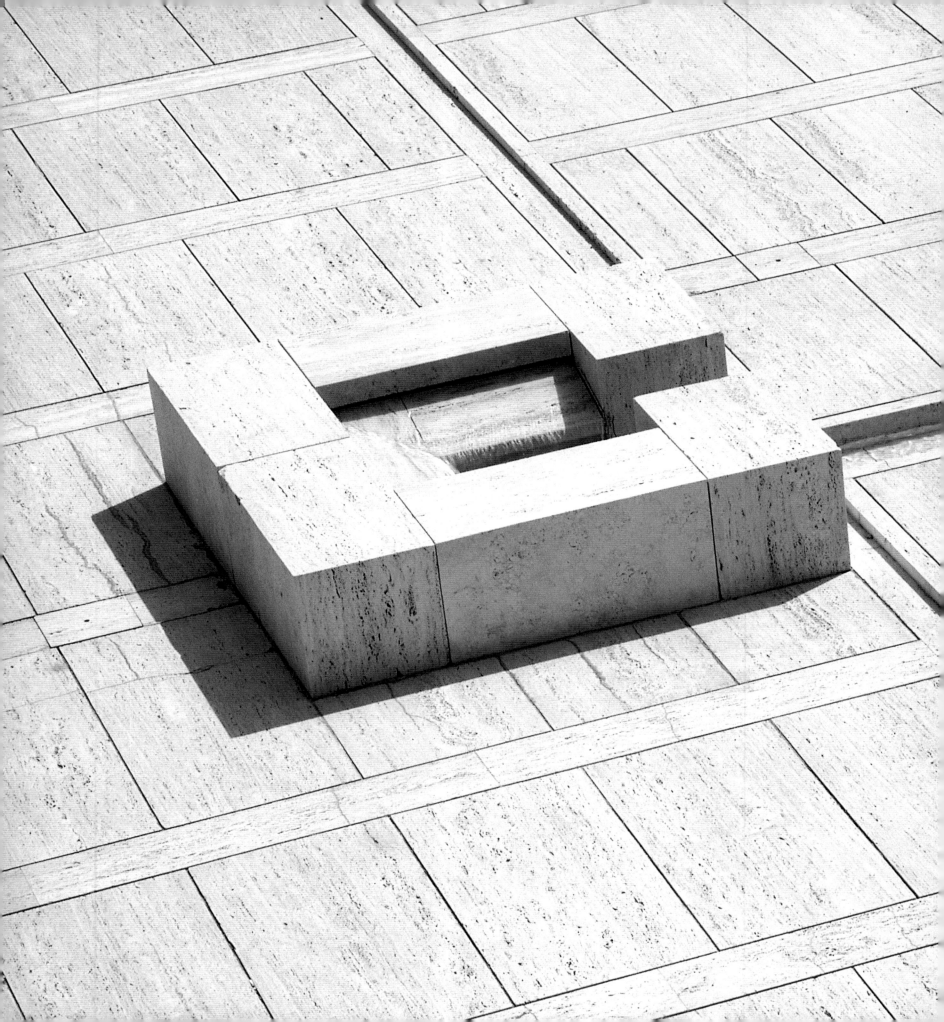

SALK
INSTITUTE
**L A   J O L L A
C A L I F O R N I A**

In *The Sacred and the Profane,* historian Mircea Eliade asserts that "men are not free to choose the sacred site . . . they only seek for it and find it by the help of mysterious signs."[1] Architect Louis Kahn's life was a quest for sacred space—space that was palpably distinct from the profane space of modern life. Ironically, he stumbled toward his most perfect realization of sacred space in a half-completed project, and some of his most trusted advisors— even after the courtyard at the Salk Institute was in place—were slow to appreciate its greatness.

The Sacred and the Profane, published in 1959, traced manifestations of sacred space throughout history and was written partly as a response to the increasing denial of ritual and myth in the modern world of rational science. Equally critical of this dilemma of modern life was C. P. Snow's *The Two Cultures,* also published in 1959, which described scientists and artists as living in two different worlds, rarely speaking to one another. The Salk Institute came into the world soon after the publication of these two books, through the efforts of two visionaries: scientist Dr. Jonas Salk, who passionately wanted to bridge Snow's two cultures, and architect Louis Kahn, who deeply believed that architecture could, in Eliade's words, "awaken individual experience and transmute it into a spiritual comprehension of the world."[2] Seldom in American architecture has there been a more perfect congruence of client, architect, project, and moment in history. The collaboration began when Salk asked Kahn to design a hundred thousand square feet of laboratory space, then electrified the architect by adding: "I would like to be able

A square fountain releases water into a four-inch channel that runs the length of the Salk Institute's travertine marble courtyard.

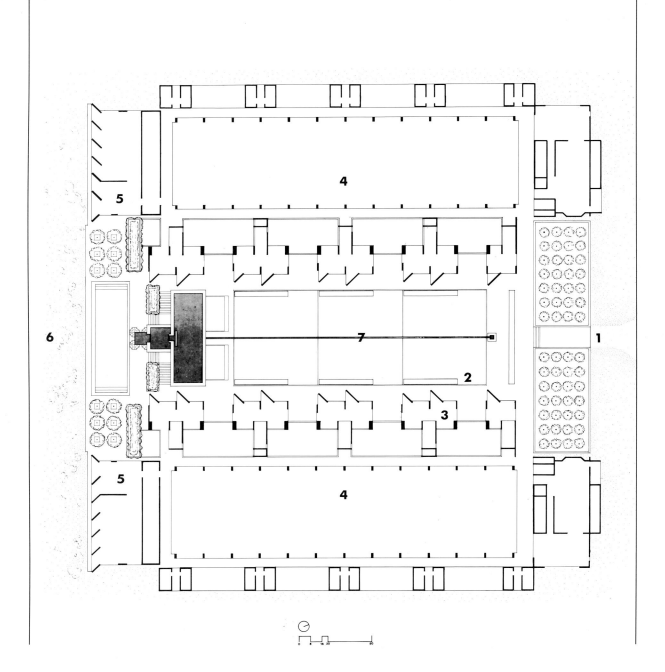

to invite my friend Picasso to the laboratories."[3]

The Salk Institute, in La Jolla, California, is a large research facility founded by Dr. Salk during the height of his fame as the conqueror of polio. In 1959 Salk commissioned Kahn to design laboratories, a large conference center (called the Meeting House by Salk and Kahn), and residences for scientists working at the Institute. Dr. Salk was drawn to California because, he felt, "A pioneering atmosphere still prevails here. The concept of an institute bringing into fusion science and the humanities is readily acceptable here."[4] The site he selected begins at the head of a ravine and fans out to either side until both the ravine and the higher, buildable areas on either side end at a steep cliff overlooking the Pacific Ocean. Salk was attracted to the site despite the problems posed by the central ravine because "the kind of institute I had in mind would be best situated at the juncture of land, sea and sky."[5]

Kahn suggested dividing the Institute into three basic programmatic elements—working, meeting, and residence—and arranging them around the ravine. Kahn sited the laboratory buildings at the

The Salk Institute seen from the site of the proposed Meeting House across the ravine.

apex of the triangle, but it was to be the Meeting House on the north side of the ravine that would welcome visitors to the Institute. Kahn was well along on plans for the Meeting House when the Institute ran short of funds and had to cancel the project. Though never built, the Meeting House is considered one of Kahn's masterpieces: a place where scientists, artists, philosophers, musicians, and other guests would gather to eat, reflect, enjoy theatrical performances and concerts, and respond to Kahn's complex and deeply spiritual architecture. In Kahn's words, the Meeting House held "unmeasurable qualities," while the laboratories were dedicated to "measurable qualities."[6]

The most unfortunate consequence of the unfinished plan is that visitors are deposited directly into the courtyard, a vast open space between the two flanking laboratory buildings. Since there are no architectural clues as to which building is one's intended destination, first-time visitors may feel as if they had accidentally stumbled into the haunting streetscape of a de Chirico painting. But if the Salk Institute fails to provide an adequate entry threshold, it is so conceptually and philosophically complete that once one becomes oriented, the disappointment of the entry sequence becomes irrelevant.

Dr. Salk compares the Institute to the human body, with the laboratories as the cerebellum, the nine-foot-deep spaces between the floors—which carry the plumbing, electrical conduits, and specialized scientific equipment[7]—as the lungs and organs, and the courtyard as the soul. Kahn spoke eloquently of an architecture of served spaces (the laboratories) and servant spaces (the utility rooms, the spaces between the floors).

It is impossible to understand the courtyard fully without these metaphorical readings of the Institute. The courtyard is where C. P. Snow's two worlds now communicate, instead of at the Meeting House, as Kahn originally envisioned. The courtyard is oriented east to west with the rising and setting sun, and the enormous phalanxes of concrete screen walls that enclose the courtyard insist that one confront the horizon. A stream of water is released from a small square fountain and runs in a four-inch channel to a wide pool, from which it then rushes through a square declivity to a pool on the terrace below, reiterating the natural axis of the ravine dividing the site. The water channel is cut into the courtyard's travertine marble floor with no edging, and in fact all the materials at Salk are solid, evident, and incontrovertible. The water in the pool at the end of the courtyard does not brim over the edge as it does in the reflecting pool at the Wright House (see pages 72–85). Kahn believed that by understanding materials and how they define space and reveal light, architecture could transcend

sty e and become as eternal as the material itself.

The courtyard is indeed the soul of the Institute, a place of perfect silence and light, imbued with what Kahn calls "a sense of wonder that precedes knowing; that precedes knowledge."[8] Some scientists working at the Salk Institute are initially intimidated by the monumentality of the courtyard, but in time find it a place to cleanse their minds and escape the pressures of their laboratory experiments. Those who prefer a view of the ravine (only the horizon of the ocean is visible from the courtyard) without the metaphysical intensity of the courtyard can descend, like the water, to the terrace, which ends at the edge of the ravine. Here there is a simple seat wall, augmented with casual chairs. At the base of the lower pool are travertine blocks with a three-quarter circle sliced off at one

corner, as if to receive the human body. While the travertine fountain in the courtyard is implosive and intense, the blocks on the terrace are expansive, relaxed. The walls of the Institute reinforce this duality—those facing east are of unfinished concrete while those facing west incorporate teakwood, which is particularly beautiful in the setting sun. As Kahn often remarked: "The sun never knew how great it was until it hit the side of a building."[9]

There have been complaints that the Salk Institute is too stark and monumental, and as it ages, the incompleteness of the master plan makes the lack of humanizing elements all the more acute. Landscape architect Lawrence Halprin, a close friend of Kahn, commented after the building was finished: "I'd seen other things of Lou's I thought were better. I didn't think [the Salk Institute] was the greatest

The courtyard in the evening.

At the end of the courtyard, the water flows into a wide pool and then into another pool on the terrace below.
OPPOSITE

thing Kahn had ever done and I especially think that paving that courtyard was the wrong thing to do."[10] Halprin and others have reached this conclusion because to them the Institute is a place where people come to work, but Salk and Kahn saw that work as an almost religious quest for the truth that would save lives (recently, Salk's search for a cure for AIDS has intensified the religious commitment of the scientists at the Institute). It is no accident that the plan for the courtyard began with Salk's memory of the cloistered garden of the church of St. Francis of Assisi in Italy[11]—which happened to be one of Kahn's favorite churches—and one can more easily imagine the Institute as a great monastery than as the kind of relaxed work environment envisioned by Halprin. Kahn's design is validated as long as the scientists who work there not only want to win the Nobel Prize but also read poetry and philosophy and appreciate the art of Louis Kahn and Pablo Picasso.

It is a perfect tribute to Kahn that one of his greatest compositions came very late in the design process, indeed after most of the laboratory was built. His love of ideas and passion for redesigning sometimes drove his associates mad—engineer and frequent collaborator August Komendant complained that Kahn never realized that a small design change often meant days of work for the engineers.[12] Kahn did not mind starting over from scratch if a better concept came into being. One of his credos was: "I honor beginnings. Of all things, I honor beginnings. I believe that what was has always been, and what is has always been, and what will be has always been."[13]

The courtyard at the Institute had many beginnings, and the story of its origins bears witness to Eliade's thesis that great landscapes come into the world in different ways, but are seldom willed solely by an individual genius. At Salk, as at the Bloedel Reserve, it was the client who provided the inspiration and the guiding vision, and the designer who gave form to that vision. Kahn acknowledged Salk's inspiration and guidance, but made it clear that he was the designer. He had maintained this distinction throughout his career: "Although collaboration in the Arts is not possible, collaboration in that which motivates the Arts is possible."[14] Salk found immense pleasure in exchanging ideas with Kahn: "And it didn't make any difference whether he came up with the idea or I did—the idea was born anyway."[15]

Three years after beginning work on the Institute, Kahn had designed four laboratories with two small courtyards between them. Just before contractors were scheduled to bid on the project, Salk felt that something was terribly wrong. After a sleepless night, he called Kahn and told him that the four buildings were destroying the sense of wholeness they were seeking. Kahn's design had been vigorously applauded by colleagues, but the architect didn't hesitate to consolidate the four laboratories into two, telling associates that Salk had given him the chance to design an even greater building.

This consolidation meant that the space between the two buildings was much larger than the previous courtyards and far more important. Kahn explained, "Two gardens were just a convenience. But one is really a place: you put meaning into it; you feel loyalty to it."[16]

Loyalty meant trying, in Kahn's favorite phrase, "to ask the garden what it wants to be." As the laboratories were being constructed, Kahn and his associates produced several different designs for the central space, but Kahn found each one unworthy of the buildings. Around this time, Kahn saw an exhibition of the work of Mexican architect Luis Barragán (1902–1989) at The Museum of Modern Art and decided to ask him to help design the space. Barragán, who surprisingly had never heard of Kahn, met with Salk and Kahn at the site. There Barragán exclaimed, " . . . not one leaf, nor plant, nor one flower, nor dirt. If you make a plaza it will unite the two buildings and it will give you a facade to the sky!"[17] It was a moment of insight for which the oxymoron "blinding clarity" was invented. Kahn and Salk instantly agreed.

After a preliminary effort to design the space together, Kahn and Barragán found that their ideas for the courtyard were aesthetically too divergent to extend the collaboration. But as Kahn developed the design of the courtyard, he incorporated Bar-

The approach to the courtyard through flanking bosques of orange trees.

The Institute's westward-facing walls incorporate teakwood. OPPOSITE

ragán's suggestion to use a water channel, both to unify the space and to solve the courtyard's drainage problems. Salk then suggested adding some benches along the side to introduce a human scale. When measuring the benches, Kahn and Salk referred to the scale of the human soul, not the human body. The benches are forty-two feet long.

The laboratories were constructed of teakwood and concrete. Kahn understood that concrete is a natural material, not synthetic,[18] and that its honeycombing and random imperfections were its natural beauty. Kahn used the retaining walls and basements of the Institute to experiment with different concrete finishes. He and Salk carefully inspected each pour and made adjustments so that by the time the walls themselves were poured, the

contractor was able to achieve an effect that Kahn described as "an order of nature . . . the marks of the concrete forms . . . make this so-called molten stone appear wonderfully capable—a product of the mind."[19]

Originally, Kahn intended to use slate for the courtyard floor, but he found an unexpected bargain in travertine that had been shipped as ballast from Italy to California. He soon realized that travertine would beautifully complement the Institute's concrete because the stone is also irregular and "The two materials give it a monolithic character."[20]

Still, Kahn and Salk were uneasy with the plaza and hired landscape architect Lawrence Halprin, who sketched out several schemes that softened the great court with evergreens and grass between

stone pavers. Halprin tried to convince Kahn and Salk that the courtyard should offer smell, sound, and all the other sensual qualities of a paradise garden, but the landscape architect soon came to realize that Kahn was obsessed with clarification and that having purified his design from four laboratories to two and two courtyards to one with all the trees and plants removed, he was not going to reverse himself and begin "enriching" the courtyard. In Kahn's mind, the courtyard had decided what it wanted to be. He later wrote: "A great building must begin with the unmeasurable and go through the measurable in the process of design, but must in the end be unmeasurable . . . what is unmeasurable is the psychic spirit."[21]

Kahn's architecture at the Salk Institute is not sculptural, but environmental. Nature—space, sky, and water—asserts itself in the courtyard. Water, the source of life, gushes forth and runs west to the void of the horizon. The enclosing wing walls enfold the courtyard, and at sunset, massive shadows spread across the travertine surface while the sky turns fiery and bold. Vibrant and resonant, the courtyard seems to summon a new harmony of science and art into the modern world. In the Salk laboratories, scientists work toward saving human lives, surrounded by architecture that affirms that human life is very much worth saving.

PROJECT: **THE SALK INSTITUTE**

CLIENT: **THE SALK INSTITUTE FOR BIOLOGICAL STUDIES**

DATE OF COMPLETION: **1965**

LOCATION: **LA JOLLA, CALIFORNIA**

ARCHITECT: **LOUIS I. KAHN ARCHITECT;** JOB CAPTAIN: **JACK MacALLISTER**

LANDSCAPE ARCHITECT: **ROLAND S. HOYT**

STRUCTURAL CONSULTANT: **DR. AUGUST E. KOMENDANT**

ASSOCIATED STRUCTURAL ENGINEERS: **FERVOR-DORLAND & ASSOCIATES**

ELECTRICAL-MECHANICAL ENGINEERS: **FRED F. DUBIN ASSOCIATES**

SITE ENGINEERS: **RICH ENGINEERING CO.**

The water channel draws the viewer's eye toward the horizon and the setting sun.

NOTES

PREFACE (p. 8)

1. Laurie Olin, "Form, Meaning, and Expression in Landscape Architecture," *Landscape Journal* 7, no. 2, Fall 1988, 166.

INTRODUCTION (pp. 10–13)

1. Fletcher Steele, "New Pioneering in Garden Design," *Landscape Architecture*, April 1930, 162–63. Despite Steele's efforts, these experimental French gardens were not widely known in the United States, though they were eagerly studied by Tommy Church, Garrett Eckbo, and other early modern landscape architects.
2. Interview with Garrett Eckbo, 17 July 1989.
3. Henry-Russell Hitchcock, Jr., "Gardens in Relation to Modern Architecture," in *Contemporary Landscape Architecture and Its Sources*, exhibition catalog, San Francisco Museum of Art, 1937, 15–19.
4. Interview with Peter Walker, San Francisco, California, 21 October 1989.
5. Interview with Stuart O. Dawson, Baltimore, Maryland, 18 November 1988.
6. Olin, "Form, Meaning, and Expression in Landscape Architecture," 152.
7. Randolph T. Hester, Jr., "Process CAN Be Style," *Landscape Architecture*, May 1983, 49.
8. Conversation with Elizabeth Meyers, 19 August 1990.
9. Telephone interview with Grady Clay, 23 July 1990.

ONE. TRADITION AND INVENTION (pp. 14–15)

1. George Kubler, *The Shape of Time: Remarks on the History of Things* (New Haven, Conn.: Yale University Press, 1962).
2. John Dixon Hunt and Peter Willis, eds. *The Genius of the Place* (Cambridge, Mass.: MIT Press, 1988), 51.

PEPSICO (pp. 17–27)

1. Elizabeth Kendall Thompson, "Suburban Office Buildings," *Architectural Record*, February 1972, 114.
2. Interview with Edward Durell Stone, Jr., 23 October 1987.
3. A "pastoral design" is one that tries to recreate the spacious, tranquil experience of idealized rural scenery. Pastoral designs usually employ broad stretches of lawn, clumps of trees, and gentle bodies of water, and their highest expression is found in the Twenty-third Psalm: "He maketh me to lie down in green pastures / He leadeth me beside the still waters."
4. Telephone interview with Donald Kendall, 22 March 1990.
5. Ibid.
6. Interview with Edward Durell Stone, Jr., 23 October 1987.
7. Russell Page, *The Education of a Gardener* (New York: Random House, 1983), 2.
8. Sidney Lawrence and George Foy, *Gardens in Stone* (New York: Scala Books, 1984), 33.
9. Telephone interview with Donald Kendall, 22 March 1990.

DEERE & COMPANY (pp. 29–39)

1. Leo Marx, *The Machine in the Garden* (Oxford, Eng.: Oxford University Press, 1964).
2. Eero Saarinen, *Eero Saarinen on His Work* (New Haven: Yale University Press, 1968), 82.
3. Deere & Company later purchased additional land for expansion and now owns over 1,200 acres.
4. William Hewitt, "The Genesis of a Great Building—and of an Unusual Friendship." *AIA Journal*, August 1977, 142.
5. "Eero Saarinen," *Architecture and Urbanism*, April 1984, 235.
6. The initial master plan, which was never carried forward, included Deere's products division in the farm fields on the other side of the highway. Its landscape design would have extended the regularity of the adjoining farm fields (also owned by Deere) into formal bosques of trees and a quarter-mile allée of sycamore trees, all of which would have been a complete counterpoint to the pastoral landscape of Deere's Headquarters.
7. Saarinen, *Eero Saarinen on His Work*, 82.
8. Edward Hall, *The Fourth Dimension in Architecture: The Impact of Building on Man's Behavior* (Santa Fe, N. Mex.: Sunstone Press, 1972), 57.
9. Correspondence with Stuart O. Dawson, 16 August 1990.
10. Interview with Stuart O. Dawson, Baltimore, Maryland, 18 November 1988.
11. Telephone interview with Stuart O. Dawson, 3 March 1990.
12. Ibid.
13. Although it looks as though the island was designed for *Hill Arches*, the sculpture was actually purchased after the island was built.
14. When landscape architect James Rose, well known for the Japanese influence on his work, was asked if he would design a Japanese garden, he smiled and said: "I'd love to. Where in Japan do you live?"
15. Conversation with Peter Walker, 23 July 1989.
16. Eero Saarinen, "Saarinen," *Perspecta* 7 (1963), 29.

WEYERHAEUSER (pp. 41–51)

1. Conversation with Peter Holland, Weyerhaeuser Company, 20 May 1989.
2. Conversation with Peter Walker, 29 October 1989.
3. Ibid.
4. Telephone interview with Danny Powell, 6 June 1990.
5. Telephone interview with E. Charles Bassett, 14 February 1990.

THE BLOEDEL RESERVE (pp. 53–69)

1. Prentice Bloedel, "The Bloedel Reserve—Its Purpose Its Future," *University of Washington Arboretum Bulletin*, Spring 1980, 3.
2. Prentice Bloedel, "Observations Expanding on the 'Statement, Nature and Purpose,' " unpublished transcript, 25 June 1977. In discussions of the Reserve, it is important to bear in mind that many Japanese gardens feature many straight paths and hard-edged rectilinear enclosures, contrary to the impression created by photographic books and by the Japanese gardens in the United States. See *Japanese Gardens* by Mitchell Bring and Josse Wayembergh for detailed plans of important Japanese gardens.
3. Ibid.

4. Prentice Bloedel served as president of the board of the Arbor Fund from its founding in 1974 until 1984, when illness made it necessary for him to name his son-in-law, Bagley Wright, as his successor.
5. Interview with Richard Haag, Seattle, Washington, 18 May 1989.
6. Bloedel, "The Bloedel Reserve—Its Purpose Its Future," 4.
7. Richard Brown, "The Central Gardens: The History, The Plantings," background information for docent tours, 10 April 1990.
8. Alders, a native tree that quickly recolonizes cleared land, is weak-wooded, often multi-stemmed, and susceptible to insects, beavers, and other pests. However, it establishes itself quickly on marginal or wet land and most species have the ability to fix nitrogen. They are widely used throughout Europe in mass plantings along highways or as windbreaks.
9. Lawrence Kreisman, *The Bloedel Reserve: Gardens in the Forest* (Bainbridge Island, Wash.: The Arbor Fund, 1988), 43.
10. Richard Brown, "The Japanese Garden: The History, the Plantings," background information for docent tours, 13 February 1990.
11. Bloedel, "The Bloedel Reserve—Its Purpose Its Future," 4.
12. Susan Rademacher Frey, "A Series of Gardens," *Landscape Architecture*, September/October 1986, 56.
13. Interview with Richard Haag, Seattle, Washington, 18 May 1989.
14. The Shorelines Management Policy prohibited building directly on the shore, so neither the beach nor the sound is integrated into the Reserve, making the property a more arboreal experience than it might otherwise have been.
15. Frey, "A Series of Gardens," 57.
16. Interview with Richard Haag, Seattle, Washington, 18 May 1989.
17. Bloedel, "The Bloedel Reserve—Its Purpose Its Future," 5.
18. These benches are so original and apt that one regrets the standard teak benches in the bird marsh and other viewing areas and wishes that an artist might be commissioned to create more site-specific seating However, the teak benches were selected by Virginia Bloedel and, for now, they are respected by the Arbor Fund as part of the legacy of the Bloedel family.
19. At the time of the engagement of EPD, the Bloedels gave Haag permission to enter the Garden of Planes, the moss garden, the reflection garden, and the bird marsh in an American Society of Landscape Architects award competition as "A Series of Gardens," without reference to the larger Reserve. Haag's entry won the President's Award of Excellence—the highest honor, and one that is not awarded each year.
20. Telephone interview with Geoffrey Rausch, 11 November 1989.
21. Virginia Bloedel passed away in 1989 and Bloedel's visits to the Reserve have been limited by his health.
22. Telephone interview with Geoffrey Rausch, 7 November 1989.
23. Ibid.

TWO. MODERN SPACE (pp. 70–71)

1. Albert Einstein, *Relativity* (New York: Random House, 1961), 9.
2. Lawrence Halprin, *Notebooks, 1959–1971* (Cambridge, Mass.: MIT Press, 1972), 64.

THE WRIGHT HOUSE (pp. 73–85)

1. Correspondence with Arthur Erickson, 10 September 1990.
2. Telephone conversation with Arthur Erickson, 3 August 1990.
3. John Charles Olmsted and Frederick Law Olmsted, Jr., sons of the designer of Central Park, Frederick Law Olmsted.
4. Arthur Erickson, *The Architecture of Arthur Erickson* (New York: Harper & Row, 1988), 42.
5. Ibid.
6. Ibid., 12.
7. Telephone interview with Cornelia Hahn Oberlander, 20 May 1990.
8. Ibid.
9. Erickson, *The Architecture of Arthur Erickson*, 43.

CIGNA (pp. 87–99)

1. Carol Herselle Krinsky, *Gordon Bunshaft of Skidmore, Owings & Merrill* (Cambridge, Mass.: MIT Press, 1988), 59.
2. Ibid., xiv.
3. One of these parking lots was replaced by a parking garage when the building was expanded in 1972. The site plan also accommodated the construction in 1981 of a large new facility that is not visible from the original building.
4. Correspondence with Paschall Campbell, 30 March 1990. Campbell notes that 1990 environmental regulations on wetlands would have prohibited draining the swamp.
5. Andrea O. Dean, "Bunshaft and Noguchi: An Uneasy but Highly Productive Architect-Artist Collaboration," *AIA Journal*, October 1976, 53.
6. Isamu Noguchi, "The Sculptor and the Architect," *Studio*, 1968, 18.
7. Telephone interview with Gordon Bunshaft, 6 June 1989.
8. Dean, "Bunshaft and Noguchi," 53.
9. Ibid., 54.
10. Telephone interview with Gordon Bunshaft, 6 June 1989.

THE DE MENIL HOUSE (pp. 101–11)

1. Peter Arnell and Ted Brickford, eds., *Charles Gwathmey and Robert Siegel: Buildings and Projects 1964–1984* (New York: Harper & Row, 1984), 9.
2. Barbaralee Diamondstein, *American Architecture Now* (New York: Rizzoli, 1980), 75.
3. Arnell and Brickford, eds., *Charles Gwathmey and Robert Siegel*, 208.
4. Telephone interview with Daniel Stewart, 7 December 1989.
5. Arnell and Brickford, eds., *Charles Gwathmey and Robert Siegel*, 211.
6. Ibid., 209.
7. David Morton, "Hampton House," *Progressive Architecture*, December 1983, 47.
8. Since today the house has cable-television service, the satellite dish is now obsolete, posing an interesting problem of historic preservation.
9. Telephone interview with Daniel Stewart, 7 December 1989.

THE MILLER HOUSE (pp. 113–27)

1. In Warren T. Byrd, Jr., and Reuben Rainey, eds., *The Work of Dan Kiley: A Diaglogue on Design Theory* (Charlottesville, Va.: Division of Landscape Architecture, The

University of Virginia, 1983), 24.

2. "A Contemporary Palladian Villa," *Architecture Forum*, September 1958, 126–31.

3. James S. Ackerman, *The Villa* (Princeton, N.J.: Princeton University Press, 1990), 107.

4. Telephone interview with Kevin Roche, 3 May 1990.

5. "Landscape Design: The Work of Dan Kiley," *Process Architecture*, no. 33 (Tokyo: Process Architecture Publishing Company, Ltd., 1982), 21.

6. The ground plane is to landscape architects what the skin of a building is to architects; it is the most important datum line and every modulation is significant.

7. Telephone interview with Mr. Miller, 23 September 1990.

8. Interview with Dan Kiley, San Francisco, California, 28 October 1990.

9. Byrd and Rainey, eds., *The Work of Dan Kiley*, 16.

10. Interview with Dan Kiley, Cambridge, Massachusetts, April 1983.

11. Interview on National Public Radio with Lee Ann Hanson, 9 December 1990.

THREE. MODERN NARRATIVES
(pp. 128–29)

1. I am indebted to Laurie Olin for this observation.

THE FULLER HOUSE
(pp. 131–41)

1. Vincent Scully, *Pueblo Mountain, Village, Dance* (Chicago: University of Chicago Press, 1989), 7–8.

2. "Antoine Predock," *GA Houses 21* (Tokyo: A.D.A. Edita, Ltd., 1987), 76.

3. I am indebted to architecture historian Kingston Heath for the term "empathetic regionalism," which he uses to describe a design rooted in the local human experiences of a region as opposed to a design that tries to replicate or blend in with existing vernacular architectural styles.

4. The concept *sol y sombra* (sun *and* shade) is central to Spanish life, the traditional *siesta* in the shade, for example, when the sun is at its peak. *Sol o Sombra* (sun *or* shade) is a phrase used to designate the seating at Spanish bullfights, where spectators can choose to buy cheaper seats in the sun.

5. Telephone interview with Antoine Predock, 4 November 1989.

6. Jay Appleton, *The Experience of Landscape* (New York: John Wiley and Sons, 1975).

7. "Antoine Predock," *GA Houses 21*, 76.

IRA'S FOUNTAIN (pp. 143–53)

1. Interview with Angela Danadjieva, Seattle, Washington, 28 October 1989.

2. Lawrence Halprin, *Cities* (Cambridge, Mass.: MIT Press, 1972).

3. "Lawrence Halprin," *Process Architecture*, no. 4 (Tokyo: Process Architecture Publishing Company, 1978), 240–42.

4. Interview with Angela Danadjieva, Seattle, Washington, 28 October 1989.

5. In 1989 an inebriated man drowned beneath one of the falls, but the police ruled it an intentionally self-destructive act and no suit was brought against the city

6. Interview with the Bureau of Risk Management for the City of Portland, 28 June 1990.

7. Economics notwithstanding, the aesthetics certainly appealed to Halprin, whose urban projects usually have far more sawed-off, broad-shouldered blocks of concrete or stone

than soft, embracing curves. In the Portland Open Space Sequence, Ira's Fountain's concrete or hard surfaces are angular and "masculine," while the earth mounds at Pettygrove Park are "feminine."

8. Wallace Stevens, "Esthétique du Mal" in *The Palm at the End of the Mind* (New York: Vintage Books, 1972), 259.

BECTON DICKINSON
(pp. 155–63)

1. Mildred F. Schmertz, "Recollection and Invention," *Architectural Record*, January 1988, 84.

2. Telephone interview with Michael McKinnell, 29 October 1990. See Mildred F. Schmertz, "A New 'House' for the American Academy of Arts and Sciences," *Architectural Record*, November 1981, for comments and sketches on the same theme.

3. Telephone interview with Andrew Leonard, project manager for Morgan Wheelock, Inc., 27 September 1990.

4. Ibid.

5. Interview with Michael Singer, 25 August 1990.

6. Telephone interview with Richard Fleischner, 16 May 1989.

7. Telephone interview with Morgan Wheelock, 19 May 1989.

8. Telephone interview with Jim McCulloch, 27 September 1990.

THE DONNELL GARDEN
(pp. 165–73)

1. Thomas D. Church, *Gardens Are for People* (New York: Reinhold Publishing Corporation, 1955), 33.

2. Ibid., 244.

3. The framing oaks died after the photographs for this book were taken, and it will be many years before their replacements achieve the same size.

4. From family recollections of the Donnell's children, Sandra D. Donnell and Bruce B. Donnell, and son-in-law Justin Faggioli, 21 July 1989.

THE CROSBY ARBORETUM
(pp. 175–89)

1. John H. Napier III, "Piney Woods Past: A Pastoral Elegy," in *Mississippi's Piney Woods*, ed. Noel Polk (Jackson, Miss.: University of Southern Mississippi Press, 1986), 23.

2. Interview with Edward Blake, Jr., the Crosby Arboretum, 16 March 1989.

3. Wallace Stevens, "The Comedian as the Letter C," in *The Palm at the End of the Mind* (New York: Vintage Books, 1972), 68.

4. William Blake and James J. Kilpatrick, *The American South: Four Seasons of the Land* (Birmingham, Ala.: Oxmoor House, 1980), xxx.

5. "Pinecote" was the name given to the Interpretive Center's pavilion by architect Fay Jones. Since "cote" is a shelter for birds, it became linked in Jones's mind with the natural shelter provided by the nearby pine trees. The name was later extended to the entire sixty-four-acre site.

6. Telephone interview with Carol Franklin, 12 May 1990.

7. The Crosby Arboretum now uses the 1,200-foot-deep well for potable water and irrigation of transplants, and to fill or flush the pond only in extreme droughts.

8. In landscape design the term "picturesque" is often used in the sense of "making landscapes like a picture by using painterly

compositional devices." A more useful and exact definition comes from eighteenth-century English writers Uvedale Price and Richard Payne Knight, who described the picturesque as a refraction of what might otherwise be seen as a whole in a landscape featuring complexity, irregularity, variation, and concealment. The path at Pinecote, which enlarges the landscape experience by concealing the whole from view, and whose ecological design features roughness and variation may be contrasted with the pastoral landscape at PepsiCo.

9. Carol Franklin, memo to the Crosby Arboretum on ecological design, 12 April 1988.

10. Frederick Steiner and Todd Johnson, "Fitness, Adaptability, Delight," *Landscape Architecture*, March 1990, 97–101.

11. From *Interpretation of the Crosby Arboretum Site*, rough draft, 1988, supplied by Edward Blake, Jr.

12. Jesse L. White, Jr. "Addressing the Consequences of Our Past," *ARBOREPORT* 3, no. 1, 1988, a report from the Crosby Arboretum.

13. Conversation with Fay Jones, Charlotte, North Carolina, 23 March 1989.

14. Ibid.

FOUR. THE ESSENTIAL FORM
PALEY PARK
(pp. 191–97)

1. Robert Zion and Harold Breen, *New Parks for New York*, exhibition catalog. Exhibition sponsored by the Architectural League of New York and the Park Association of New York, Inc., 1963, unpaginated.

2. Interview with Robert Zion, 23 August 1987.

3. William H. Whyte, *City* (New York: Doubleday, 1988), 140.

4. Zion and Breen, *New Parks for New York*, unpaginated.

5. Antoine Grumbach, "The Promenades of Paris," *Oppositions* 8 (Spring 1977): 51.

6. Interview with Hideo Sasaki, 7 August 1988.

7. Ada Louise Huxtable, "Experiment in Parks," *The New York Times*, 2 February 1966, 37.

8. Interview with Robert Zion, 23 August 1987.

9. Zion and Breen, *New Parks for New York*, unpaginated.

GAS WORKS PARK
(pp. 199–207)

1. Telephone interview with Richard Haag, 27 September 1990.

2. Craig Campbell, "Seattle's Gas Plant Park," *Landscape Architecture*, July 1973, 343–49.

3. Telephone interview with Richard Haag, 27 September 1990.

4. Telephone interview with Ernie Ferrero, 28 August 1990.

5. J. William Thompson. "Landscape of Dream. Warrior of Vision," *Landscape Architecture*, September 1989, 86.

6. Sally Woodbridge, "In Search of a Place to Play," *Landscape Architecture*, May 1990, 68.

7. Kenneth E. Read, "The Ghostly Gas Works," *Seattle Magazine*, November 1969, 42–45.

THE TANNER FOUNTAIN
(pp. 209–15)

1. Lucy Lippard, *Overlay* (New York: Pantheon Books, 1983), 39.

2. Jayne Merkel, "Beyond Harvard Yard," *Landscape Architecture*, March/April 1987, 66.

3. Interview with Peter Walker, Cambridge, Massachusetts, 20 July 1988.

4. Conversation with Peter Walker, San Francisco, California, 22 October 1989.

5. What in previous years would have been an impossible maintenance task—cutting the grass around the base of boulders—is now routine thanks to the humble nylon grass whip.

6. See Peter Walker and Cathy Deino Blake, "Minimalist Gardens Without Walls," in *The Meaning of Gardens*, eds. Mark Francis and Randolph T. Hester, Jr. (Cambridge: Mass.: MIT Press, 1990), 120–30.

7. For a more extended discussion of the relationship of the Tanner Fountain to *Stone Field Sculpture*, see Jory Johnson, "The Presence of Stone," *Landscape Architecture*, July/August 1986, 64–69.

8. In his seminal essay on minimalist art, art critic Michael Fried argues that the "theatrical" nature of minimalism that Walker extends in his designs, is in fact "the negation of art" because it denies the art's objecthood. See Michael Fried, "Art and Objecthood," in *Minimal Art: A Critical Anthology*, ed. Gregory Batcock (New York: E. P. Dutton & Co., 1968).

9. Yogi Sasaki, ed. "Peter Walker: Landscape as Art," *Process Architecture*, no. 85 (Tokyo: Process Architecture Publishing Company, 1989), 25. In the next breath, Walker undercuts this definition by admitting that viewing gardens are "functional," thereby endorsing a definition of function that might include any work of art.

10. Ralph Waldo Emerson, "The American Scholar," in *Selected Prose and Poetry* (New York: Holt, Rinehart and Winston, 1950), 65.

VIETNAM VETERANS
MEMORIAL (pp. 217–25)

1. When she won the competition, Maya Lin was not a registered architect. The architect of record for the Memorial is the Washington-based firm of Cooper-Lecky, for whom Lin was officially a consultant.

2. Telephone conversation with Maya Lin, 28 November 1989.

3. Martin Heidegger, *Poetry, Language, Thought*, trans. Albert Hofstadter (New York: Harper Colophon Books, 1971), 154.

4. Previous war memorials with massive lists of names, such as the Memorial to the Missing of Somme, listed the names in alphabetical order. Lin's chronological order makes it difficult to find specific names and the Vietnam Veterans and Park Service set up locational directories near the Memorial. Part of the present emotional experience of the Memorial is the awareness of people *searching* for names, a process that would take far less time if they were in alphabetical order.

5. From the concept statement submitted by Maya Lin as part of the competition submission. In *The Experimental Tradition*, ed. Hélène Lipstadt (New York: Princeton Architectural Press, 1989), 124.

6. Many more additions have been proposed since the Vietnam Veterans Memorial opened, but for the foreseeable future, they will not be contiguous to the wall.

7. For an elaboration on the respective meanings of Hart's and Lin's memorials, one of the best discussions is in William Hubbard, "A Meaning for Monuments," *The Public Interest*, Winter 1984, 17–30.

8. Telephone conversation with Maya Lin, 28 November 1989.

9. Lawrence B. Anderson, ed., *Process in*

Architecture: A Documentation of Six Examples (Cambridge, Mass.: MIT Press, 1979), 46.

10. Lin, who was an undergraduate architecture student at Yale when she designed the Memorial, says she was inspired by architectural historian Vincent Scully's lecture on these two memorials.

11. From the concept statement submitted by Maya Lin as part of the competition submission. In The Experimental Tradition, ed. Hélène Lipstadt, 124.

12. Saint Ignatius of Loyola, Anchor Anthology of 17th Century Verse, vol. I, ed. L. Martz, (New Haven, Conn.: Yale University Press, 1954), 27.

SALK INSTITUTE (pp. 227–35)

1. Mircea Eliade, The Sacred and the Profane (New York: Harcourt Brace & World, Inc., 1959), 28.

2. Ibid., 51.

3. John Lobell, Between Silence and Light: Spirit in the Architecture of Louis I. Kahn (Boulder, Colo.: Shambhala Publications, Inc., 1979), 76.

4. Esther McCoy, "Dr. Salk Talks About His Institute," Architectural Forum, December 1967, 27.

5. Ibid., 28.

6. Richard Saul Wurman, What Will Be Has Always Been: The Words of Louis I. Kahn (New York: Access Press Ltd., 1986), 23.

7. Thanks to these deep spaces, the Salk Laboratories had no problems integrating computers—the kind of retrofitting that has vexed many older research facilities.

8. Louis Kahn, "I Love Beginnings," A + U: Louis I. Kahn, 1965, 279.

9. Ibid., 284.

10. Wurman, What Will Be Has Always Been, 279.

11. McCoy, "Dr. Salk Talks About His Institute," 30–31.

12. August Komendant, 18 Years with Architect Louis I. Kahn (Englewood, N.J.: Aloray Publishers, 1975), 61.

13. Louis Kahn, "1973: Brooklyn, New York," Perspecta: The Yale Architectural Journal, vol. 19, 98.

14. Wurman, What Will Be Has Always Been, 210.

15. Ibid., 296.

16. Ibid., 280.

17. Ibid., 269.

18. Nor is concrete a "modern" material. It was the most characteristic building material of the Romans, though subsequently it was almost forgotten and seldom used until the late eighteenth century. It didn't become a dominant material again until the early twentieth century.

19. Wurman, What Will Be Has Always Been, 241.

20. Ibid.

21. Ibid., 262.

SELECTED BIBLIOGRAPHY

WORKS ON AMERICAN LANDSCAPE DESIGN SINCE WORLD WAR II

Abercrombie, Stanley. "Evaluation: A Prototype Left Unreplicated." Architecture, December 1985, 54–55.

Bye, A. E. Art into Landscape, Landscape into Art. Mesa, Ariz.: PDA Publishing Corporation, 1983.

"American Landscape Architecture." SD (Space Design) 88:08.

Byrd, Warren T., Jr. "Comparative Anatomy." Landscape Architecture, March 1983, 54–58.

———, ed. The Work of Garrett Eckbo. Charlottesville, Va.: University of Virginia, 1987.

Chabrier, Yvonne V. "The Greening of Copley Square." Landscape Architecture, November/December 1985, 70–76.

Church, Thomas. Gardens Are for People. 2nd ed. New York: McGraw-Hill, Inc., 1983 (see also first edition, 1955).

———. Your Private World: A Study of Intimate Gardens. San Francisco: Chronicle Books, 1969.

Collins, Lester, and Thomas Gillespie. Landscape Architecture (exhibition catalog). Cambridge, Mass.: Harvard University Graduate School of Design. 1950.

Condon, Patrick Michael. "Cubist Space, Volumetric Space, and Landscape Architecture." Landscape Journal, Spring 1988, 1–14.

Condon, Patrick M., and Lance M. Neckar, eds. The Avant-Garde and the Landscape: Can They Be Reconciled? Minneapolis: Landworks Press, 1990.

Eckbo, Garrett. Urban Landscape Design. New York: McGraw-Hill, Inc., 1964.

———. Landscapes for Living. New York: Architectural Record with Duell, Sloan & Pearce, F. W. Dodge Corp., 1950.

———. The Landscape We See. New York: McGraw-Hill, Inc., 1969.

Freeman, Richard B., ed. Landscape Design (exhibition catalog). San Francisco Museum of Art, 1948.

Frey, Susan Rademacher. "A Series of Gardens." Landscape Architecture, September/October 1986, 54–61, 128.

"Garrett Eckbo: Philosophy of Landscape."

Process Architecture, no. 90. Tokyo: Process Architecture Publishing Company, 1990 (entire issue devoted to Eckbo).

Halprin, Lawrence. Changing Places. San Francisco: San Francisco Museum of Modern Art, 1986.

———. Notebooks: 1959–1971. Cambridge: MIT Press, 1972.

"Houses and Landscapes." Progressive Architecture, May 1960, 141–79.

Howett, Catherine. "New Directions in Environmental Art." Landscape Architecture, January 1973, 39–46.

———. "PepsiCo Reconsidered." Landscape Architecture, April 1989, 82–85.

———, ed. Abstracting the Landscape: The Artistry of Landscape Architect A. E. Bye. University Park, Penn.: Pennsylvania State University, 1990.

Howland, Joseph E. The House Beautiful Book of Gardens and Outdoor Living. New York: Doubleday & Company, Inc., 1958.

"How We Build: The Values That Shape Our Environment." Conference proceedings, The University of Virginia School of Architecture, Charlottesville, Va., 1989.

"The Inhabited Landscape: An Exhibition." Places 4, no. 4.

Jellicoe, Geoffrey, and Susan Jellicoe. Modern Private Gardens. London: Abelard-Schuman, 1968.

Jewell, Linda, ed. Peter Walker: Experiments in Gesture, Seriality and Flatness. New York: Rizzoli, 1990, 14–20.

Johnson, Jory. "Pastures of Plenty." Landscape Architecture, March 1990, 50–58.

Kassler, Elizabeth. Modern Gardens and the Landscape. Rev. ed. New York: The Museum of Modern Art, 1984.

Krog, Steven R. "The Language of Modern." Landscape Architecture, March/April 1985, 56–59.

Landecker, Heidi. "Profile: Carol Johnson." Landscape Architecture, June 1989, 80–86.

"Landscape Design: The Work of Dan Kiley." Process Architecture, no. 33. Tokyo: Process Architecture Publishing Company, 1983 (entire issue devoted to Kiley).

"Lawrence Halprin." Process Architecture, no. 4. Tokyo: Process Architecture Publishing Company, 1985 (entire issue devoted to Halprin).

Leccese, Michael. "John Simonds Orients His Work to Stir the Senses." Landscape Architecture, March 1990, 78–83.

———. "Canadian Modern." Landscape Architecture, December 1989, 64–69.

MacFadyen, J. Tevere. "Russell Page at PepsiCo." Horticulture, July 1986, 30–44.

McHarg, Ian L. Design with Nature. New York: Doubleday & Company, Inc., 1969.

Messenger, Pam-Anela. "El Novillero Revisited." Landscape Architecture, March 1983, 54–67.

Meyer, Elizabeth K. "The Modern Framework." Landscape Architecture, March/April 1983, 50–53.

"Modernism." Landscape Architecture, January 1990 (entire issue devoted to modernism).

Montgomery, Robert. "A Building That Makes Its Own Landscape." Architectural Forum, March 1972, 20–27.

"M. Paul Friedberg: Landscape Design." Process Architecture, no. 82. Tokyo: Process Architecture Publishing Company, 1989 (entire issue devoted to Friedberg).

Olin, Laurie. "Form, Meaning, and Expression in Landscape Architecture." Landscape Journal, Fall 1988, 149–68.

Posner, Ellen. "Harmony, not Uniqueness." Landscape Architecture, May 1989, 42–49.

Roche, Mary. "The Lines and Textures of Nature." House Beautiful, April 1951, 107–13.

Rowan, Jan C. "Design of Exterior Spaces." Progressive Architecture, July 1960, 108–26.

Rose, James. Creative Gardens. New York: Reinhold Publishing Corporation, 1958.

Sasaki, Yogi, ed. "Peter Walker: Landscape as Art." Process Architecture, no. 85, Tokyo: Process Architecture Publishing Company, 1989 (entire issue devoted to Walker).

Shirvani, Diane Wilk. "Church, Aalto and Cubism: Modern Eclecticism in Landscape Architecture." Avant-Garde 2, Summer 1989, 62–77.

Simo, Melanie. "Hideo Sasaki." Pacific

Horticulture, Winter 1988, 16–25.

Snow, Marc. Modern American Gardens—Designed by James Rose. New York: Reinhold Publishing Corporation, 1967.

"SOM's Landscape Architecture." Progressive Architecture, June 1962, 132–43.

Streatfield, David C. "Where Pine and Palm Meet: The California Garden as a Regional Expression." Landscape Journal, Fall 1985, 61–74.

Temko, Allan. "Evaluation: Louis Kahn's Salk Institute After a Dozen Years." AIA Journal, March 1977, 42–48.

Thompson, J. William. "Profile: Richard Haag." Landscape Architecture, September 1989, 80–87.

Tunnard, Christopher. Gardens in the Modern Landscape. 2nd ed. New York: Charles Scribner's Sons, 1948.

Van Valkenburgh, Michael R. Built Landscapes: Gardens in the Northeast. Brattleboro, Vt.: Brattleboro Museum and Art Center, 1984.

Weisskamp, Herbert. Beautiful Homes and Gardens in California. New York: Harry N. Abrams, Inc., 1964.

INDEX

Italic page numbers refer to captions and illustrations.